Complete Book
OF

Wedding
Showers

by
Diane Warner

CAREER PRESS
3 Tice Road, P.O. Box 687
Franklin Lakes, NJ 07417
1-800-CAREER-1; 201-848-0310 (NJ and outside U.S.)
FAX: 201-848-1727

DIANE WARNER'S COMPLETE BOOK OF WEDDING SHOWERS
ISBN 1-56414-300-7, $11.99
Cover design by Tom Phon
Typesetting by Eileen Munson
Printed in the U.S.A. by Book-mart Press

To order this title by mail, please include price as noted above, $2.50 handling per order, and $1.50 for each book ordered. Send to Career Press, Inc., 3 Tice Road, P.O. Box 687, Franklin Lakes, NJ 07417.
Or call toll-free 1-800-CAREER-1 (NJ and Canada: 201-848-0310) to order using VISA or MasterCard, or for further information on books from Career Press.

Library of Congress Cataloging-in-Publication Data

Warner, Diane
    [Complete book of wedding showers]
    Diane Warner's complete book of wedding showers: hundreds of creative shower ideas / by Diane Warner.
         p.   cm.
    Includes index.
    ISBN 1-56414-300-7 (pbk.)
      1. Showers (Parties)   2. Weddings.   I. Title
GV1472.7.S5W37   1998
793.2–dc21   97-41431
                                                    CIP

❧❧

To my husband,

Jack,

for his encouragement,

support, and patience.

❧❧

Many thanks to all of you who agreed to share your party ideas with my readers, with special thanks to Janice Burroughs, Michele Perry, Lisa Warner, Lynn Paden, and Roy and Linda Glass.

I am also grateful to my editors at Career Press—Betsy Sheldon, Eileen Munson, and Regina McAloney—for their help in putting together this book.

∂•∝

Other Wedding Books
by Diane Warner

How to Have a Big Wedding on a Small Budget

*Big Wedding on a Small Budget
Planner and Organizer*

*Beautiful Wedding Decorations and Gifts
on a Small Budget*

*How to Have a Fabulous, Romantic
Honeymoon on a Budget*

*Picture-Perfect Worry-Free Weddings:
71 Destinations & Venues*

The Best Wedding Ever

Complete Book of Wedding Vows

Complete Book of Wedding Toasts

CONTENTS

Introduction

How *did* this tradition of showering the happy couple with gifts before their wedding day begin? Legend has it that it began with a romance in Holland many years ago between a beautiful young girl and an impoverished miller. The miller, as the story goes, was so poor he could not provide the young woman with anything in the way of worldly goods, and he thus incurred the disdain of the girl's father. The father would not accept the man as his daughter's husband and attempted to sabotage the marriage by refusing to hand over his daughter's dowry. Some local villagers, however, took pity on the couple and "showered" them with a community dowry. And so, today we bestow many gifts upon those who are dear to us before their wedding day—whatever their financial status may be.

Who usually hosts a wedding shower? Traditionally, the bride's honor attendant or her bridesmaids do, but nowadays friends, co-workers, and relatives are taking on this role more and more. In fact, it is not unheard of for several people—couples in the apartment complex where the bride or groom lives, a singles group in which the couple met, a group of women from the bride's church—to do the honors. Even the bride's mother or sister is an acceptable hostess, departing greatly from old-fashioned rules of etiquette that discouraged such a thing.

What *hasn't* changed about the individual who hosts the party, however, are the categories into which the person usually falls. As I researched for this book, I discovered that three types of hostesses are prevalent:

The natural hostess. This type of person loves to entertain and can organize a party seemingly without effort. Blessed with the gift of hospitality, this hostess knows instinctively what needs to be done to plan any type of celebration.

The reluctant hostess. This type of person is practically pushed to maximum stress overload by the thought of attending a party, much less *hosting* one. This person is none-too-thrilled about adding party planning to an already demanding schedule.

The willing hostess. This type of person (like me) doesn't mind hosting a shower, as long as she knows how to go about it and has plenty of time to plan in advance.

Whatever category you fall into, I have good news for you: You'll find this book filled with fresh new ideas guaranteed to make your party a success and easy worksheets to keep you organized as you plan the event.

If you make the most of the tips and suggestions offered here, you just might come off like a "natural" after all!

ᴥPART Iᴥ

Planning the Party

The next eight chapters serve to give you a crash course—"Party Planning 101." They will help you determine:
- What kind of party you would like to host.
- How to delegate some of the duties.
- Where the party will be held.
- Who to invite and what type of invitations you will send.
- How to decorate the party site.
- What kinds of games you will play.
- How you will entertain your guests.
- How you will toast the happy couple.

One important tip: Plan a party that's not only fun for your honored guest but for you as well! If you take on more than you can handle, you'll feel stressed and your guests will sense it. Remember, "shower" isn't synonomous with "grand affair." Cleverly coordinated invitations, name tags, favors, themes, color schemes, decorations, food, games, and entertainment are all very nice and are all covered in this book, but don't feel guilty if you decide to host a very informal party, using only one or two of my ideas. Plan the type of party that feels good for you, and everyone will enjoy it!

CHAPTER 1

୬

Preparing Yourself

Before You Rush Out and Buy the Streamers...

You're probably already anxious to get started on the preparations for your party. Before you launch into your party plans, however, a few things require your consideration:

- What type of hostess are you—reluctant, willing, or that rare and wonderful "natural" who can plan the entire party while you're folding your laundry?
- How much time and money are you able to spend on the party preparations and the party itself?
- Is the bride getting married for the first time, or has she been married before?
- Who will be invited to your party? Will it be co-ed?
- Where will the party be held?
- How many guests can you accommodate?

- Will the party be formal or informal?
- Will the guests "watch" or "participate"?
- What day and time would be best for everyone?
- Are there others who would like to co-host this party?
- What theme or activities would be most appropriate for the bride or groom and the guests?

Jot down your answers and keep them in mind as you read through the ideas in this book. Before you pondered these questions, you may have envisioned a riotous party around the pool with plenty of fun, games, and a live rock band, but you may now realize perhaps this is not at all appropriate for the bride's elderly grandmothers and great-aunts. On the other hand, you may not want to plan a party that's too formal and rigid, especially if the guests will be mixed singles and younger married couples who are looking to have a good time.

Then there are the problems of time and money. Not all parties are created equal. Some are more complicated to plan and more expensive to pull off than others. One way around time and money constraints is to delegate. Perhaps you could find others who would love to co-host the party, sharing the costs and responsibilities. This is an especially good idea if several people were already thinking of hosting their own party for the couple, because it would eliminate overburdening the guests with invitations to numerous parties for the same couple.

What if your answer to the first question was "reluctant"? Well, there's always the informal party. This type of party takes practically no planning at all and very little in the way of expense. For example, it could be an office party. In that case, picking a good time to have it is pretty simple—it could be held during the lunch hour, right after work, or during a long coffee break. The decorations can be as uncomplicated as a balloon bouquet and the food as hassle-free as cake and coffee. The important thing is that the bride or couple feel loved and honored and are "showered" with thoughtful gifts.

Sometimes an informal party is the preferred way to go, especially if the bride-to-be has been married before. She was probably "showered" several times over the first time around. What she needs now is to feel the love and support of her closest friends and family members, along with gifts of a more personal nature because she probably has most of her household necessities.

Now, let's discuss one of the very first decisions you'll have to make: *when* to hold the shower.

How to set the date

A good rule of thumb: Hold the shower *four to five weeks before the wedding*. A lot of stress is involved in planning a wedding, so the last thing you want to do is plan a party too close to the couple's wedding day. A month or so before the wedding is best, if you can get your plans to come together by then.

Here are some other factors that should go into establishing a party date:

Let the bride set the actual date. It's a *really* good idea for the bride to be present at her own party, so be sure to check with her first.

Be sure the date doesn't conflict with another party. Call around to see if your date will conflict with any other party being hosted for the couple. Or ask the bride—she should certainly know.

Choose a date that is convenient for your guests. Give some thought to your guests' schedules, too. If most of them work Monday through Friday, a weekend party may be best.

Choose an appropriate time of day. Choose a time that is best for the guest of honor as well as yourself. After all, you need plenty of time to clean, decorate, and prepare the food. Choose a time that is suitable for the theme of the party and the type of food you will be serving. Here are some general guidelines:

Breakfast: between 8 and 10 a.m.

Brunch: between 10 a.m. and 1 p.m.

Luncheon buffet: between 12 noon and 2 p.m.

Formal tea: beginning at any time between 2 and 3:30 p.m.

Dinner party: between 6 and 8 p.m.

Dessert party: any time after dinner.

How to delegate

In addition to setting the date and time, you will need to start thinking about delegating some of the party-planning duties to other people.

Whether you ask others to co-host the party or you decide to host it by yourself, you will still need help to keep everything running smoothly. Here are a few of the responsibilities that can be delegated to others:

- Compiling the guest list, including addresses and telephone numbers.
- Addressing invitations.
- Making decorations, name tags, place cards, and favors.
- Cooking or baking some of the food.
- Decorating.
- Arranging the gifts.
- Recording the gifts (item and name of donor) as they are opened.
- Passing the gifts around the room for all the guests to see, being sure greeting cards stay with their corresponding gifts.
- Fashioning gift ribbons into "pretend bouquets" to be carried by the bride and her attendants during the rehearsal.

- Recording the bride's exact comments about each gift (see "The Wedding Night" in Chapter 7).
- Placing instant photos in an album to be given to the bride.
- Conducting games, if any.
- Introducing the entertainment, if any.
- Serving the food and drink.

Know your limits

The chapters that follow will help you determine the important components of planning and hosting a successful wedding shower, including location, theme, menu, and budget.

One thing to keep in mind as you read these chapters: Know your own personal limitations. If you've never prepared and served a sit-down dinner for 15 couples before, don't try it now. Or if the thought of serving a formal bridal tea scares you to death, don't even consider it!

Remember, plan the type of party that's comfortable for you and within the limits of your expertise and the amount of your free time.

CHAPTER 2

~

Picking the Theme

From Formal Tea To Harley Party

The best part of planning a wedding shower is choosing a theme for your party. It will get you into the spirit and make the planning easier than you expected. It will help you coordinate the invitations, decorations, party favors, and, of course, the food. In fact, once you've chosen your theme, you'll find that it carries itself along, practically planning the party for you.

As you consider the various themes described in this chapter, give some thought to the bride and groom and choose a theme that suits their personalities. Also consider the guests: Are they already acquainted with each other, or will this be the first time many of them have met? What are their ages? Some themes lend themselves to mixed-age groups; others are more suitable for the couple's immediate peers.

By the way, you don't have to implement a theme *exactly* the way it's described here. You can mix and match ideas, plus add a few personalized touches of your own. For example, the "Amateur Night" theme I suggest for a "his-and-hers" party can also be used for an engagement party, at which some of the older relatives could be talked into performing.

I have rated each party theme on a scale of one to five in terms of its formality (represented by a heart symbol), its cost (represented by a dollar sign), and the level of stress involved (represented by an exclamation mark). The more symbols—the higher the formality, cost, or stress level. Please don't let these ratings intimidate you, however, because you can always ask for help when it comes to the planning. For example, if your party will be a very expensive affair, such as a formal sit-down dinner, you may want to enlist several co-hosts who are able to help out with the costs. Likewise, if a certain party theme involves a lot of complicated planning and "doing" to pull it off, you may want to lower the stress factor by delegating some of the duties.

Have fun as you consider the themes here. I'm sure you'll find one that's just right for your party.

Engagement parties

The purpose of an engagement party, of course, is to celebrate the couple's engagement, but it is also a chance for the two families to meet and get to know each other. It can be a formal or informal get-together and may be hosted and attended by either friends or family. Traditionally, however, it has been a formal party hosted by the bride's or groom's parents and attended by members of the couple's families.

In any case, there are two general guidelines to follow when planning an engagement party:

1. Choose a theme that is appropriate for couples.

2. Discourage intimate gifts (this is no time to "shower" the bride with lacy negligees or the groom with something more appropriate for a bachelor party).

Elegant, Sit-Down Engagement Dinner

Formality	♥ ♥ ♥ ♥ ♥
Cost	$ $ $ $ $
Stress	! ! ! ! !

This party is limited to members of the bride's and groom's families, many of whom have probably never met each other. The menu is usually quite elaborate and served via "plate service" or "French service" (see Chapter 10). The meal may have many courses, so the dining takes up most of the evening. Therefore, the party becomes a "talk party," as opposed to a "game party," and the entertainment may be limited to the bride and groom telling the story of their courtship: how they met, how he proposed, their wedding plans, and so forth. In addition, professional musicians, such as a stringed trio, may perform while the guests are being served. If you really want to impress your guests as they enjoy their after-dinner coffee, you can arrange for a soloist or instrumentalist to perform a short "concert." Also, Chapter 5 gives centerpiece and decoration ideas suitable for this type of party, including napkin folding and using place cards.

By the way, if the bride and groom come from very large families, you may want to consider a more affordable theme, such as the "meet the family" picnic described later in this chapter.

Tip: Hire a limousine to transport the happy couple to and from your party site.

Candlelight-and-Roses Dessert Party

Formality	♥ ♥ ♥
Cost	$ $ $
Stress	! ! !

This is an excellent choice if you would like to host a formal party but don't have the time or funds to plan a sit-down dinner. The ambiance is created with candles, fresh or silk roses, and lots of swirling tulle netting and delicate ribbons. You can add a little more light, as well, by stringing tiny white Christmas lights along the tables, around the plants or garlands, and over doorways. This theme works best, of course, as an evening affair. Because this is also a formal party, you may want to limit the entertainment to soft background music and good conversation, which is what the guests often prefer if they are trying to get to know each other.

In addition to serving your own personal favorites, you can try some of the delicious desserts for which I've provided recipes in Chapters 9, 10, and 11 as well as the dessert-type drinks described in Chapter 12.

If you like the idea of a dessert party but would like to host something less formal, you can use less elaborate decorations and include any of the games or get-acquainted activities described in Chapter 6.

A Country Garden Party

Formality	♥ ♥ ♥
Cost	$ $
Stress	! !

This theme works best outdoors in an actual garden setting. You could, however, hold it indoors and create a fake garden setting by decorating the site with pots of real and artificial flowers, silk ficus trees, park benches, birdbaths filled with floating candles and gardenias, a white trellis entwined with paper flowers, a low white picket fence, and patio tables with umbrellas and set with potted geraniums. You can serve a formal afternoon tea (see Chapter 10) or a luncheon buffet (see Chapter 9).

Country-Western Barbecue

Formality	
Cost	$ $ $
Stress	! !

Drag out your cowboy boots, 10-gallon hats, and bandannas for this party. Decorate with lariats, cowboy hats, saddles, branding irons, potted cactus plants, hay bales, and red-checkered tablecloths. Rent a dance floor if necessary and provide live or taped music for a little country-western dancing after you eat. By the time your guests have done a couple of line dances, they will be into the spirit of the party and will be entertaining themselves!

See the "Barbecue Bash" menu in Chapter 9.

"Remember When...?" Party

Formality	♥ ♥
Cost	$ $ $
Stress	! !

Collect memorabilia from the couple's past to use as decorations: baby pictures, Little League uniforms, cheerleading pompons, old high school or college yearbooks, scrapbooks, pennants, awards, trophies, etc. Dress up two teddy bears as a bride and a groom (preferably the bride's and groom's own childhood bears, if they still exist). Create a veil for the bride bear out of white tulle netting and a top hat for the groom bear from black construction paper. (It doesn't matter if the top hat and veil aren't perfect; it's the thought that counts!)

If the party is attended by members of the couple's families who have never met, set up a photo corner—an area displaying the wedding photographs of the bride's and groom's parents, grandparents, aunts and uncles, or brothers and sisters. This nostalgic corner will be a focal point throughout the party as relatives from both sides gather around to compare wedding fashions and to talk about their own engagements and wedding ceremonies. You may even be able to add a display of wedding memorabilia, such as the grandmothers' wedding gowns, fans, shoes, hair combs, or bridal veils. If possible, model the gowns on a dressmaker's form or mannequin.

The main entertainment can be a "Remember when...?" slide or video show (see Chapter 7). You can serve any of the informal menus in Chapter 9 or the ethnic menus in Chapter 11.

A Toasting

Formality	♥ ♥
Cost	$ $
Stress	! !

Instead of a roasting, host a "toasting"—a trendy, informal theme centered around wines, cheeses, and related gifts. The hosts furnish a selection of cheeses, plus a couple of cheese boards, a supply of plastic wine glasses, paper plates, and napkins. Really a very simple menu!

The invitation, which can be designed to resemble a wine label, will request that each guest bring two bottles of wine—one for tasting and one as a gift—along with any wrapped wine or cheese-related item. Gift ideas may include a corkscrew, a pair of wine glasses, a cheese cutter, or even a wine-making kit. By the way, encourage any teetotalers to bring a nonalcoholic wine or champagne. A wine rack will serve as a practical table decoration that can be used to display the gift bottles until they are unwrapped.

In addition to bringing gifts, the guests are asked to come prepared to toast the couple. Their toasts can be serious, reminiscent, or humorous. It is hoped they will be varied, interesting, and entertaining, because they will serve as the main entertainment of the evening. The toasts in Chapter 8 are appropriate for this party as well, but for anyone who needs a little help composing a toast, you may want to suggest my book, *Complete Book of Wedding Toasts.*

If you, as the host or hostess, compose a special, personalized toast ahead of time, which is a good idea anyway, a nice gift might be to have a calligrapher write your toast on a piece of parchment paper, which can be framed and presented to the couple as a memento of the party.

Tip: As a responsible host, you may want to go easy on the tasting yourself so that you'll be available to drive anyone home who may have had a few too many "sips."

Hawaiian Luau

Formality	♥ ♥
Cost	$ $ $
Stress	! !

Here is another easy party to put together. All you'll need are a few tiki torches, grass skirts, ukuleles, flower leis, and, if you happen to have a pool, a floating raft filled with bright paper or fresh flowers. This is a "hang-loose," relaxed sort of party, so do everything you can to make the guests feel comfortable: Wear a Hawaiian sarong or shirt, furnish the guests with fresh flower or synthetic leis, and have plenty of soothing Hawaiian music playing in the background.

Of course, the success of a luau depends on the quality of the food and the way it's presented. There is a complete luau menu included in Chapter 9.

"Meet the Family" Picnic

Formality	
Cost	$
Stress	!

If the bride and groom both come from large families and there will be quite a crowd at your party, why not make it a good old-fashioned potluck picnic? You will have plenty of room for everyone, and there will be very little expense involved. You can reserve a designated area in a local park, rent a private park, or hold it in the backyard if there's enough room.

All you'll need in the way of decorations are a couple balloon bouquets, which can be tied to the ends of the picnic tables, and a watermelon centerpiece (insert fresh cut flowers into the flesh of a watermelon that has been cut in half). If the guests will be bringing gifts, place them in a large decorated laundry basket. Set the tables with the usual red and white checkered tablecloths, bring several ice chests full of drinks, and let the party begin.

You might want to play one of the get-acquainted games described in Chapter 6, followed by a few old-fashioned picnic games, which are fun for everyone but especially for great-aunts and great-uncles, grandparents, and any other older folks who remember them with fondness. Here a few examples of these traditional favorites:

- Nail-pounding contest
- Wheelbarrow race
- Sack race
- Kick-the-shoe contest
- Horseshoe toss
- Egg toss or water balloon toss
- Three-legged race

Tip: Not all guests may bring gifts to the engagement party, so you may want to have the couple open the gifts after the party so that those who didn't bring gifts won't be embarrassed.

"His-and-hers" showers

The key to a successful his-and-hers shower is to keep it lively and interesting by getting everyone involved. The themes that follow emphasize fun and participation. As far as the food goes, you can serve the special menu suggested as part of the theme itself, or you can serve any of the informal menus suggested in Chapter 9.

Amateur Night

Formality
Cost $
Stress   ! ! !

Remember the best thing about summer camp—the talent show, at which kids performed skits, sang, played instruments, told jokes, recited a silly poem, or demonstrated some amazing "one-of-a-kind" feat? Well, that's the idea behind this theme.

Try to remember some of the crazy, bizarre things you used to do when you were in high school and college—the sillier, the better. For example, one amateur night party I attended featured three guys who sang their own version of "I Left My Heart in San Francisco," using a karaoke machine. They had rewritten the lyrics to tell the story of how the bride and groom met, and it was hilarious—especially because none of the three could carry a tune! Then six of the gals came out to compete in a hula hoop contest, followed by a band that performed with kazoos, sandpaper blocks, a broomstick bass, pots as drums, lids as cymbals, and a "musical saw." Every guy in the band wore a ridiculous hat and kept a straight face during the "performance," which added to the humor all the more. To top it all off, there was a master of ceremonies, complete in tux and top hat, who introduced each act as seriously as possible. It was great!

If you really want to go all out with this idea, you can set up chairs in a theater-in-the-round setting with a raised stage. Darken the room and have ushers use flashlights to lead guests to their seats. You can also set up a cardboard "laugh-o-meter" and turn the arrow up by hand, according to the amount of applause each act receives, and then give awards for "best musical group," "most creative," etc. You can even hand out programs to the guests as they are seated, featuring humorous background sketches of each of the performers. You can serve bags of buttered popcorn and large-sized drinks during the performances, followed later in the evening with a make-your-own-ice-cream-sundae buffet.

Just remember that what makes one of these parties a success is to incorporate as much humor as possible. This is not the time for a serious piano recital. It's all tongue-in-cheek—as light and silly and fun as can be!

Progressive Dinner

Formality   ♥
Cost $
Stress   !

This is a practical and affordable way for several couples to co-host a co-ed shower. A progressive dinner, of course, is one in which the guests travel from home to home, eating one course at each. The couples get together to plan the menu and decide on the decorations.

The dinner can be formal or informal, served on elegant china or paper plates. The menu may be frugal or gourmet, sit-down or buffet, ethnic or standard fare. In addition to the recipes suggested later in this book, you may also want to include a few of the ideas from Chapters 5 and 6 once guests have settled in at the final destination.

Harley Party

Formality
Cost $-$ $ $ $
Stress   !

If your bride and groom are into Harley-Davidson motorcycles, nothing would please them more than a Harley party.

If the party is being hosted by fellow Harley buffs, it can be included as part of an all-day or weekend Harley run, which can be quite costly. You can opt for a simple, affordable Harley party by decorating with Harley posters, toy Harleys used as centerpieces or cake decorations, etc.

Encourage the guests to come dressed in their motorcycle gear and to bring Harley gifts, which can be found in profusion at any Harley shop—saddlebags, chaps, T-shirts, canteens, vests, jewelry, grills, double sleeping bags, etc.

Hard Hat Shower

Formality	
Cost	**$ $**
Stress	**! !**

This is a perfect party for the couple who have already purchased or who plan to purchase their own home. The guests are asked to wear "work grubbies" to the party, including well-worn jeans, T-shirts, workboots, eye goggles, toolbelts, and hard hats (or painting caps or straw gardening hats). Encourage the guests to bring their gifts "wrapped" in their original bags from the store, tied with colorful rope or string.

Decorate the shower site with plumbers' helpers (toilet plungers) spray-painted in bright colors and adorned with "ribbons" made from bright plastic surveyor's tape. Fill a small paint bucket with fresh flowers, and embellish it with paint brushes, stir sticks, and paint color sample cards.

The hosts of the party may want to buy a wheelbarrow as their gift to the couple, which can serve as the main decoration as well. As the guests arrive, ask them to place their gifts in the decorated wheelbarrow. For entertainment, you can ask the guests to describe their worst home repair disasters, or you can include one or two of the games described in Chapter 6, such as

"The Liar Game." The object of this shower is to furnish the couple with things they will need for their new home, such as a hammer, screwdrivers, a measuring tape, saws, pruning shears, a lawn edger, flower seeds, gardening tools, a broom, a shovel, ladders, an electric sander, a drill, hooks, screws, nails, and any of the hundreds of other things sold in a hardware store.

"Down-and-Dirty" Party

Formality	
Cost	**$-$ $ $ $**
Stress	**!**

This party is similar to a "Hard Hat Shower," but instead of arriving in their hard hats and "pretend" work grubbies, the guests come prepared to actually *work*. In other words, this is a party in which everyone pitches in to help the couple fix up or spruce up their future home. Everyone brings all the tools they'll need—paintbrushes, shovels, hammers, saws, or wallpapering equipment.

In addition to the tools, the guests are asked to bring casseroles, salads, desserts, and drinks for the party that will follow the "workday." The guests' real gift is their elbow grease, plus any building materials they would like to contribute to the cause, such as wallpaper, unfinished wooden shutters, or buckets of paint. As hostess, all you'll need to bring are a few simple decorations, plus disposable tablecloths, tableware, trash bags, and plenty of extra ice for the drinks.

Tip: You can always order pizza to be delivered at "quitting time."

Johnny-Come-Lately Shower

Formality	♥
Cost	$ $
Stress	! !

The concept of this shower is really very simple. It is a bridal shower in which the men arrive *after* the gifts have been opened and just in time for the most important part of the party: *food!* This idea works best when there is something fun for the guys to do during the first part of the party, such as watching Monday night baseball or football in another room, playing a game of volleyball or horseshoes in the backyard, renting a movie, or going to the movie theater.

Junk Drawer Shower

> **Formality**
> **Cost** $
> **Stress**   !

Not only is this a lighthearted, fun theme, but an affordable one as well.

Every couple needs a "junk drawer" full of small tools and gadgets, all of which are absolutely crucial to running a happy home. You can use an actual drawer (from your own kitchen or workbench) to hold the gifts, and you can decorate with items from your own junk drawer, such as a small hammer, screwdrivers, a wire clipper, a flashlight, or a roll of electrical tape, and the gifts can be of the same type, just as long as they're small enough to fit into a drawer.

For entertainment, you may want to play the "Communication Game" described in Chapter 6, using junk drawer goodies to form the pattern. Or you can play "The Liar Game," with the emphasis on strange-looking items you might find in a junk drawer.

A Pound of This—A Pound of That Shower

> **Formality**   ♥
> **Cost** $ $
> **Stress**   ! !

Use an old-fashioned balance scale as the foundation for your floral centerpiece. Each guest brings a "pound of something" as a gift. For the bride: flour, sugar, coffee, salt, dried herbs, tea, bath crystals, potpourri, etc. For the groom: nails, toggle bolts, golf tees, pretzels, mixed nuts, popcorn, etc. In addition to a pound of something, ask the guests to bring enough nonperishable food to stock the couple's pantry for their first week or two of married life.

Christmas in July Party

Formality	♥ ♥
Cost	$ $ $
Stress	! !

The object of this party is to give the couple a head start on their supply of Christmas decorations for their home, yard, and Christmas tree. It's easy to decorate for one of these parties. If it is, in fact, December, and you've already decorated your home for Christmas, you won't need to add a thing. If the party is in July or another month, you'll need to drag your Christmas boxes out of storage and spread a few decorations around, including an artificial tree if you have one. You can tie ribbons in the bride's wedding colors around its branches and wrap it in garlands of popcorn you have strung in advance. As the guests arrive, their gifts can be placed under this tree. Then, as they are opened, any gifts such as ornaments or tree trimmings can be displayed on the branches. If you don't have a tree, the gifts can be stashed in a huge white cloth "Santa's pack" or inside a cardboard box that has been wrapped with Christmas paper.

And if you're one of those organized people who has saved last year's Christmas cards, you can cut them up and glue the pieces to homemade invitations, name tags, or place cards.

Basket Shower

Formality	♥
Cost	$ $
Stress	! !

This is one of the easiest themes because baskets are so plentiful. Use them to decorate the room, arranging them in clusters in the room's corners, or on the serving table along with baskets to hold the food dishes themselves.

The guests are requested to bring basket gifts, such as:

- A gourmet food basket filled with nonperishable food items.
- A honeymoon picnic basket filled with paper or plastic plates, cups, utensils, red and white checkered cloth and napkins, plastic wine glasses, beef jerky, cookies, caramel corn, cheeses, candies, plus a bottle of wine or champagne.
- A beach basket filled with beach towels, a bottle of sunscreen, a waterproof plastic camera, plastic sports bottles, a Frisbee, matching visors, etc.
- Barbecue basket filled with barbecue tools, a meat thermometer, an apron, tongs, skewers, a grill brush, etc.
- A gardening basket filled with gardening tools, gloves, seed packets, flower pots, etc.
- A game basket filled with simple board games, plus a couple of decks of cards and score pads.

Tip: Some of these gifts can be pretty pricey, so several guests may want chip in on one.

Organizer Shower

Formality	♥
Cost	$ $
Stress	! !

This type of shower is really appreciated because, more often than not, the newlyweds will be living in cramped quarters, whether an apartment, a condominium, or a small home. Anything that will help them stay organized and make the most of their space will be a great gift, such as closet organizers (garment, shoe, handbag, or sweater organizers; hat boxes; shelves) or garage organizers (peg boards for tools and supplies, or containers for nails and screws).

Cutlery Shower

Formality	♥
Cost	$ $
Stress	! !

This is an especially good idea for the couple who has been married before or has been living on their own for a while, because you can never have enough good-quality cutlery. There are dozens of gift ideas, including a cake cutter, a meat slicer, peelers, a cheese knife, a pie server, kitchen shears, utility scissors, pinking shears, cuticle scissors, a nail clipper, a can opener, a knife sharpener, an electric carving knife, steak knives, pruning shears, a butcher knife, butter spreaders, etc. A clever decoration would be an enormous pair of wooden scissors (the type used to cut ceremonial ribbons), which you could make out of plywood or cardboard.

"My Funny Valentine" Shower

Formality	♥ ♥
Cost	$ $
Stress	! !

This is an obvious, easy-to-arrange theme, especially if the party will be held during February when the Valentine's Day decorations you would need are found everywhere! (If not, cut large hearts out of red, white, and pink construction paper, and add a few heart-shaped balloons, crepe paper streamers, and white wedding bells.) Make this an evening affair, and you can cast a romantic glow around the room with pink and white candles and small white Christmas tree lights. Serve a heart-shaped cake, along with decorated heart-shaped cookies and red punch, and don't forget dreamy background music, such as Roberta Flack's "The First Time Ever I Saw Your Face" and Tony Bennett's "My Funny Valentine." Pin red carnations on the guests as they arrive, along with bright pink name tags, which will add to the party's "loverly" ambiance. Use children's valentines as place cards.

As part of the evening's entertainment, ask the bride and groom to tell their love story—how they met and fell in love and all the juicy details of the wedding proposal! A Valentine's party is a popular theme for a newly engaged couple—you can't go wrong if you choose this one!

Amusement Park Party

Formality
Cost $
Stress

As you can imagine, an afternoon at an amusement park (or a county fair) is low on stress and formality. For the hostess who is short on time and money, this is a great choice; despite the small amount of planning everyone has a good time. This is a pay-your-own-way affair for the guests, not only to get into the amusement park itself but for the meal that follows (a picnic with food from the concession stands or a fast-food meal in a nearby park). During the meal gifts are given, and the couple is toasted with paper cups. All you'll need to provide in the way of decorations are paper tablecloths, napkins, and a balloon bouquet for the picnic. And the only food you'll need to provide for the guests is a decorated cake.

Skandifest

Formality	♥ ♥ ♥
Cost	$ $ $
Stress	! ! !

Food is the highlight of any Scandinavian party, so why not plan a smorgasbord? You can make it a potluck meal to cut down on costs, but if you do you'll need to assign the dishes so there won't be duplications. A complete smorgasbord menu is included in Chapter 11.

Decorate the buffet table with a miniature Viking ship or small, wooden Swedish horses. If the couple comes from a Scandinavian background, it may be possible to borrow decorative items from their relatives, such as a Swedish apron (which can be worn by the hostess), traditional table runners, a Viking hat, and colorful posters or wall hangings.

Perhaps one or two of the older couples may be able to perform a folk dance in costume, or several of the couple's female relatives may agree to model their wedding gowns. Someone can tell the story of the "Burning Love" food dish (see the smorgasbord menu in Chapter 11). Legend says that this Danish potato casserole was created by a bride-to-be as a surprise for her bridegroom. He was so impressed not only by the tastiness of the dish itself but by her loving thoughtfulness that he carved her heart-encased initials into a tree trunk to demonstrate his "burning love" for his bride and her potato casserole. After this story, the groom may present his bride with a log that he has carved in advance with her initials surrounded by a heart. This will become a cherished momento of the party and their love for each other.

A smorgasbord can be "dressed up or down," depending on whether it is an evening or afternoon affair and depending on how formal you would like it to be.

Oktoberfest

Formality	♥
Cost	$ $ $
Stress	! !

An Oktoberfest in February? Sure, or any other month of the year! An Oktoberfest is just a chance to celebrate with plenty of German food and fun. Ask around for a few souvenirs from Germany, such as cuckoo clocks, beer steins, Hummel figurines, and so forth. And while you're at it, scout out some accordion music, and if the couple are of German heritage, you might even be able to talk some of their older relatives into wearing their authentic costumes and dancing the polka. See Chapter 11 for an authentic Oktoberfest menu.

Mexican Fiesta

Formality	♥
Cost	$ $ $
Stress	! !

A fiesta is easy to plan any time of the year, but if the party is close to the *Cinco de Mayo* (the fifth of May), all the better. This theme, of course, lends itself to Mexican food (see Chapter 11), as well as inexpensive, stress-free decorating. Piñatas, serapes, and bright paper flowers can be found at your local import shop or a party supplies store. Or if you can locate a Mexican grocery, pick up a few "miracle candles"—those wonderful, tall candles that sit inside a painted glass. You can also drag out everything you can find that's red, white, and green (the colors of the Mexican flag), and the food dishes themselves will also add color to your party.

For some background music, track down an album featuring Herb Alpert and the Tijuana Brass, or purchase one of the many great mariachi tapes or CDs on the market. Of course, if you want to do it up in a big way, hire some mariachi singers to serenade while your guests enjoy the feast.

Italian Pasta Party

Formality	♥ ♥ ♥
Cost	$ $ $
Stress	! ! !

Give your setting the feeling of an intimate Italian restaurant by decorating with red and white checkered tablecloths, plenty of candles placed in wine bottles "dripping" with wax, plus travel posters donated by your friendly travel agent. If the party is held after dark, all the better! Just turn those lights down low, light the candles, and be sure to "decorate" the pasta dishes with miniature Italian flags. A couple of Italian cuisine ideas are found in Chapter 11.

"When Irish Eyes Are Smiling" Party

Formality	♥ ♥
Cost	$ $ $
Stress	! ! !

Go crazy with St. Patrick's Day decorations. Shamrocks cut out of green construction paper can be used to decorate the party site *and* the invitations, name tags, or place cards. Also, you might want to add this to your invitations: "Wear green or you'll get pinched." If you feel especially in the spirit, create a Blarney Stone for all the guests to kiss—haul the biggest rock you can carry in from your yard and set it on a bed of crushed green tissue paper. As for entertainment, try a sing-along of Irish favorites, including "Oh, Danny Boy" and "When Irish Eyes Are Smiling." Another entertaining idea is a limerick-writing contest. Use the examples in Chapter 6 to whet your guests' creative appetites. Then award prizes for "Funniest," "Most Creative," and so forth. An Irish menu is included in Chapter 11.

Far East Feast

Formality	♥ ♥ ♥
Cost	$ $ $
Stress	! ! !

The food will be the big attraction at this party (see the menu and recipes in Chapter 11), but you can add to the ambiance with decorations, either borrowed or purchased from an import store.

If your feast is held outdoors, string Japanese or Chinese lanterns around the patio, along with Japanese fishing balls and nets. Create a Japanese garden by adding a fountain, little bridges, and potted Oriental shrubs and plants.

For an indoor party, string lanterns around the room, or cover your own fixtures with Chinese paper lamp shades. Sprinkle the room with colorful Tientsin kites, painted bamboo wall hangings, and handpainted fans.

For your centerpiece, fill a wooden cricket house with fresh or silk flowers. Play Japanese koto music or other Oriental music softly in the background.

By the way, because most of the recipes described in Chapter 11 can be cooked in a wok, you can turn the get-together into a "participation party" by letting the guests chop and stir-fry the food for the various dishes. If you decide to do this, furnish guests with white aprons (make them yourself, if you wish) on which they can write with felt-tip markers—have them write their names along with their personalized congratulations to the couple or a humorous word of advice. Their aprons will take the place of name tags.

Bon Voyage! Shower

Formality	♥ ♥ ♥
Cost	$ $ $
Stress	! ! !

This is another great idea for the couple who already "has everything," either because they've been married before or because they've already set up house and have most of the basics. Use the couple's honeymoon destination as the party's theme. If they're going on a cruise, for example, go to your travel agent and beg for cruise posters and colorful brochures.

If they're flying to Hawaii, go with a luau theme by decorating with tiki torches, conch shells, and fresh flowers. Be sure to encourage the guests to wear their "aloha shirts" and muumuus. A complete luau menu is described in Chapter 9. Or if Mexico is their destination, you can serve Mexican food, and so forth. Round up CDs and tapes of the music of their destination, such as calypso music for a Caribbean honeymoon, Hawaiian music for a luau, of course, and Mexican music for a cruise to Acapulco.

Encourage guests to bring practical travel gifts or gifts that reflect the honeymoon destination. Some ideas: film, travel iron, sewing or first aid kit, travel alarm, suntan lotion, luggage cart, plastic rain jackets, matching sun visors or swim towels (personalize them by writing their names using a liquid embroidery pen), underwater goggles, etc. Some *group* gift ideas: a travel kit filled with currency from the country the couple will be visiting, a piece of luggage, or the beach basket described for the "basket shower" earlier in this chapter.

Home from the Honeymoon Shower

Formality	♥ ♥ ♥
Cost	$ $ $
Stress	! ! !

This type of shower is perfect for the couple who eloped, had a very informal private wedding, or got married at their honeymoon destination—and it should be held as soon as possible after they return. Especially in the case of an elopement, the couple probably didn't have any pre-wedding parties. Therefore, this "home from the honeymoon" shower can have two purposes: to celebrate the marriage and to "shower" the couple with wedding gifts.

Let the honeymoon destination inspire your decorating ideas. (See the previous theme.) In any case, be sure you have at least one "welcome home" poster, preferably one they can see as they arrive. You can also use toy airplanes, cars, or boats as table decorations, depending on their mode of travel.

Other "his-and-hers" party themes to consider:

• Hobby Shower	• Halloween Costume Party
• Beach Party	• Gift Certificate Shower
• New Year's Eve Party	• Roaring 20s Shower
• Hot Tub Party	• Scavenger Hunt
• Treasure Hunt	• Theater Party
• Miniature Golf Party	• Winery Tour
• Tacky Party	• Carnival
• Elvis Party	• Renaissance Festival
• Mardi Gras Party	

Bridal Showers

The purpose of a bridal shower is to "shower" the bride with affection, support, and thoughtful, loving gifts. This section describes one formal shower theme (the formal bridal tea) and serves up several informal themes that are fun, relaxed, and easy to plan. For food ideas, consult any of the informal menus in Chapter 9 or one of the ethnic menus in Chapter 11.

Formal Bridal Tea

Formality	♥ ♥ ♥ ♥ ♥
Cost	$ $ $
Stress	! ! ! !

Let's begin with the most elegant of all bridal showers—the formal bridal tea. I'm not talking about "high tea," which is actually a hearty supper served around 6 p.m., but the "quite proper" afternoon tea. The tradition of this formal afternoon tea began in the mid 1800s when the Duchess of Bedford asked her maid to serve her miniature finger sandwiches and tiny cakes with her afternoon tea "just to tide her over until supper."

Since that time, women have come to love this type of occasion because it gives them a chance to dress to the nines and indulge in fine, cultured social interaction. A formal tea also gives us an opportunity to sample some of the traditional British tea-time treats, such as scones, tarts, trifles, and pastry puffs.

Pull out your embroidered lace tablecloths, napkins, china tea sets, and sterling silver and use them to decorate your serving table, along with old-fashioned, loosely arranged bouquets of roses and wildflowers. Also, round up as many antique dolls as you can find and set them at a miniature table with their own miniature tea set. Teddy bears will add to the decor as well; just tie lace ribbons around their necks. You can also display old wedding portraits of grandparents, and instead of a corsage, present the bride-to-be with an old-fashioned bouquet.

By the way, formal afternoon teas don't usually include "entertainment" as such, because the pleasant conversation, lovely decorations, and tasteful gifts are all the party needs to be a success. Lovely British tea-time specialties are described in Chapter 10, along with spiced pears, cold cheeses and meats, hot-cross buns, chocolate-dipped fresh strawberries, roasted nuts, and chocolate truffles.

Because it's a tea party, tea-related gifts are definitely in order, including lace tablecloths, a tea set, china or crystal serving platters, or tea cup and saucer sets. Heirloom gifts would also be nice (see the "Family Treasures" shower description that follows). Any fine gift inspired by the bride's gift registries would be appropriate as well, such as a cut crystal vase, picture frame, or sugar and cream set.

Tip: It is a time-honored formal bridal tea tradition for the bride's maid or matron of honor to pour the tea. If she isn't in attendance, the hostess may pour the tea.

Apron Shower

Formality	♥ ♥
Cost	$ $
Stress	! !

Set a freestanding coat rack near the front of the room. Decorate the top of the rack with ribbons and balloons, and create an attractive display of aprons, with cooking utensils or recipe cards protruding from their pockets. Or you can build a "lady's maid" (described in Chapter 5).

When you mail the party invitations, be sure to enclose recipe cards to be filled out and tucked into the pockets of the aprons that are brought as gifts. These recipe cards will be placed in a decorated recipe box that will be presented to the bride during the party. If you are asked for gift ideas, you can suggest lacy half-aprons, floor-length party aprons, barbecue aprons, bib aprons with humorous sayings, and sewing or gardening smocks.

And if you want your hostess gift to be something really special, you can provide a white organza apron to be autographed by all the guests, using a liquid embroidery pen (or a pencil if the signatures are to be embroidered with thread at a later date; be sure to have an embroidery hoop on hand to stretch around the fabric as it is autographed).

One of my close friends was given an autographed apron at one of her bridal showers many years ago, and to this day it is one of her most cherished possessions.

Gourmet Cooking Shower

Formality	♥ ♥ ♥
Cost	$ $
Stress	! ! !

Decorate the room with anything cooking-related, such as chef's hats, a cookbook display, a decorated recipe box, hanging braids of garlic or "bouquets" of kitchen utensils. Also, use colorful dish towels instead of a tablecloth for your serving table.

In addition to any games you might decide to play, ask each guest to tell about her worst cooking disaster. (Everyone has at least one!) Also, invite each guest to autograph an apron, as suggested above.

Family Treasures Shower

Formality	♥ ♥ ♥
Cost	$ $
Stress	! ! !

This is an intimate family shower at which the gifts are precious family heirlooms being handed down to the bride by her older female relatives. As the bride opens each gift, the donor is encouraged to tell about the gift—its age, when it came into the family, and how it was used through the years.

Ask the bride's relatives to bring their wedding gowns and wedding photos to the party. The photos can be arranged on card tables covered with old-fashioned white lace tablecloths, and the gowns can be displayed on mannequins, dressmaker forms, or pretty hangers. Or better yet, see if you can talk the bride's mother, aunts, or grandmothers into modeling their gowns in a fashion show. If anyone has "outgrown" her gown, perhaps a daughter or a niece will agree to model it instead.

Honeymoon Trousseau Shower

Formality	♥ ♥ ♥
Cost	$ $
Stress	! ! !

This is a popular theme for the bride and guests alike. The gifts are as much fun to shop for as they are for the bride to receive. This shower calls for decorations that are lacy, dainty, and feminine, such as miniature nosegays tied with ribbons, embroidered table scarves, and bouquets of fully bloomed roses. And because the theme has to do with the bride's trousseau, the gifts can be placed inside an open hope chest, in a small antique chest of drawers, or inside a miniature hope chest that can be created by covering a rectangular box with wood-grained adhesive paper, ribbons, and lace. Again, a fashion show is in order. Perhaps a local lingerie store will provide merchandise to be modeled by their staff or by guests who have agreed to it ahead of time.

If you're asked for gift ideas, suggest that the guests visit their local Victoria's Secret where they'll find dozens of beautiful things for the bride's trousseau, such as lace-top stockings, teddies, and sheer satin floats. Or you may suggest trousseau accessories, such as a fancy shower cap, peach hyacinth body splash, or scented sachet bags to tuck into her suitcase as she packs for her honeymoon.

Tip: Be sure to include the bride's lingerie sizes on the invitation.

Linen Shower

Formality	♥ ♥
Cost	$ $
Stress	! !

A simple clothesline and clothespins serve as the shower's decorations. As the bride opens her gifts (sheets, towels, etc.), they are hung on the clothesline, along with their corresponding greeting cards.

Specify on the invitation the size of the couple's bed(s), the colors of their bedroom, kitchen, and bath(s), and the size and type of their dining room table. Also, list the names of any stores where they have registered for linens. Many gifts qualify as "linens"—sheets, pillowcases, blankets, towels, bath mats, tablecloths, place mats, napkins, beach towels, guest towels, pillows, mattress pads, and dresser scarves.

"Yes, You Can" Shower

Formality	♥
Cost	$
Stress	! !

This is an upbeat, lighthearted theme with a practical twist: The guests bring packaged mixes or prepared foods—straight off the grocery store shelves—along with the pans, baking dishes, muffin tins, whisks, mixing spoons, or whatever is needed for preparing the dish.

Here are a few examples of shower gifts:
- Muffin mixes with a muffin tin
- Cookie mixes with a cookie sheet
- Corn bread mixes with a corn pone pan
- Waffle mix with a mixing bowl
- Coffee cake or any kind of cake mix with a cake pan
- Brownie mix with a square baking pan
- Scalloped potato mix with a glass baking pan
- Spaghetti noodles, canned spaghetti sauce, and Parmesan cheese with a colander

You can use some of the decorating ideas suggested for the "gourmet cooking" shower above.

Have Party, Will Travel Shower

           Formality

           Cost   **$**

           Stress   **! !**

Is the bride enrolled in an aerobics class three nights a week? Or is she a member of a bowling team? A book club? Whatever she's involved in during the week, bring the party to one of her meetings as a surprise shower. Let the leader of her group know that you'll be "bringing a party" to their meeting on a certain date, and try to keep the plans a secret if you can. Of course, the members of the group will need to be in on the surprise! The decorations can be as simple as a balloon bouquet and the food as easy as a bakery cake and a beverage. The main thing is that the bride feels honored and is "showered" with thoughtful gifts from her peers.

This is a great party idea for the hostess who doesn't have the time or money to plan a more formal affair, and it's perfect for the type-A, workaholic bride who never has a spare minute!

Recipes for Two Shower

           Formality   ♥ ♥

           Cost   **$**

           Stress   **! ! !**

This shower is fun for the guests because they get to show off some of their clever "cooking for two" ideas by bringing their prepared dishes to the party. The dishes are served with their recipe cards displayed in front of each one. Not only will the bride love these practical gifts, but the guests will enjoy the "tasting," as well. In fact, you'll need to have an extra package of index cards on hand because the guests will want to copy down each others' recipes.

Obviously, this is an affordable party to host because you will only need to provide rolls, beverages, and an extra dessert or two. Decorate by placing your own cookbooks on display, along with an attractive recipe box, which can be given as a gift to the bride. By the way, be sure to enclose a recipe card with each party invitation so that the cards will all be the same size and look nice when placed in the box.

Baskets for the Bride Shower

Formality	♥ ♥ ♥
Cost	$ $ $
Stress	! ! !

This is the same as the "basket shower" described earlier except that the gift baskets are personalized especially for the bride rather than intended for the bride and groom both. Each guest may bring a gift basket, or—because some gift baskets may be a little pricey—several guests may want to chip in on one. Here are a few gift baskets that are appropriate for a bridal shower:

- Tea-time basket filled with a teapot, a variety of teas, a jar of honey, etc.
- Bath basket filled with a loofah, bubble bath, bath oils, etc.
- Stationery basket filled with thank-you notes, writing paper, envelopes, pens, stamps, an address book, etc.
- Laundry basket filled with detergents, bleach, spot remover, a clothesline and clothespins, spray starch, etc.

Not Your Average Coffee Break Shower

Formality	♥
Cost	$ $
Stress	!

An office party takes very little in the way of planning, decorating and expense. It's the thought that counts! Set out extra-special bakery treats in one of the meeting rooms or in someone's office, decorate with a simple balloon bouquet, and invite the bride for an extended coffee break. It doesn't get much easier than that!

Another option is to bring the party to a nearby restaurant where everyone can order their lunch "Dutch Treat." Or how about ordering box lunches from a local deli that can be carried to a nearby park?

To tell the truth, anything you plan is guaranteed to be a success because *everyone* would rather party than work!

Special Times Shower

Formality	♥ ♥
Cost	$ $
Stress	! !

The theme of this party is *time*. So, when you prepare the party invitations, assign a specific day of the week, a specific month, or a time of the day to each guest, with a request that each brings a gift suitable for her "assignment." For example:

- 7 a.m.—coffee mug and bag of gourmet coffee beans.
- October—Halloween decorations for the home or yard.
- 11 p.m.—a "husband" for reading in bed or an eyeshade.
- Monday—a basket of detergents, spot removers, etc., for "laundry day."
- July—swim fins, a beach towel, a Frisbee, suntan lotion.
- September—bamboo garden rake for the fall leaves.
- 5 p.m.—cassette tapes or CDs to play in the car on the way home from work.

Also, ask each guest to wear something appropriate, as well. For example, "October" might wear a Halloween costume and "11 p.m." a nightie, etc. Encourage the guests be as creative as possible with their gifts—and a sense of humor will help make the party a success, as well.

Decorate with calendars, clocks and datebooks, plus anything cute and clever that pertains to certain months, such as children's valentines for February or a Happy New Year banner for January, etc. And if you happen to have a grandfather's clock or a cuckoo clock that can be moved into the room and decorated for the occasion, that may be the only decoration you'll need.

"Shower" Shower

Formality	♥ ♥
Cost	$ $
Stress	! ! !

For one of these showers to be successful, you need to know the couple's color preferences for their bathroom(s), which should be noted on the party invitation along with any stores where the couple has registered.

As a table centerpiece, you can fill a large decorated wicker basket with soaps, bubble baths, bath oils, loofah sponges, washcloths, etc., which can then be given to the bride later as your gift. Once you know the couple's colors, gift shopping can be a lot of fun because there are so many clever new things on the market, such as shower caddies; coordinated sets of soap-dishes, toothbrush holders, and drinking glasses; hanging or standing bathroom shelves; towel trees; digital scales; inflatable bath pillows; plastic tub trays for books and toiletries; decorative jars and bottles; tissue box covers; retractable clotheslines for the tub, etc. Group gifts may include more expensive items, such as an electric toothbrush system or a whirlpool tub attachment.

Paper Shower

Formality	♥ ♥
Cost	$ $
Stress	! !

This is a fun idea, especially for the guests, who will get a kick out of searching for unusual gifts made out of paper. Enclose a paper doll with each party invitation for the guests to "clothe" in anything that's paper and bring to the party. Award prizes for the silliest, most creative, or most bizarre paper dolls.

A clever table centerpiece might be a decorated Easter basket filled with dollar bills (everyone's favorite kind of paper, right?). Of course, all the decorations should be made out of paper—colorful paper tablecloth, paper plates, paper flowers, crepe paper streamers, etc.

If you're asked for gift ideas, you can suggest paper picnic supplies, guest towels, place mats, decorative paper tablecloth and napkins, gift wrap or gift bags, stationery, playing cards, books, message pads, shelf paper, mailing labels, computer or fax supplies, address book, and note cards. Believe it or not, there are even paper bikinis. (I received one as a gift many years ago, but I've never had the nerve to try it out! The bride might be a little more daring.)

Bridesmaids' luncheon

At last we come to the traditional bridesmaids' luncheon, which differs from the typical bridal shower for several reasons: First of all, the guests are a select group usually composed of the bride and her attendants. Gifts are almost always exchanged during this luncheon, which is commonly held about a week before the wedding. It may be hosted by *either* the bride or the bridesmaids, although usually the bride's honor attendant (maid or matron of honor) arranges it. If the bride hosts the luncheon, she picks up the tab for the meals and presents each of her attendants with a gift (usually jewelry to be worn during the wedding, such as matching pearl necklaces). If the bridesmaids host the get-together, they usually share the cost of their joint gift for the bride and the expense of the luncheon, whether it takes place in a restaurant or a private setting. Their gift, by the way, is usually something for the bride to wear on her wedding day or something personal for her to take with her on her honeymoon. (Another variation is for the cost of the luncheon to be shared equally by all the women, usually a "Dutch Treat" affair at a restaurant.)

A sentimental tradition at this affair is to serve a pink cake with trinkets hidden between its layers. The single woman whose slice contains, say, a ring is said to be the next to wed, and the one who finds a dime will become rich, and so forth.

Tip: In some parts of the country, and within certain ethnic groups, it is considered proper etiquette to invite the mothers of the bride, groom, flower girl and ring bearer, the sisters of the bride and groom, and the flower girl herself if she is old enough to enjoy the party.

Other themes to consider:

* Hobby Shower
* Home Office Shower
* "A Day at the Spa" Getaway
* Beach Party
* Gift Certificate Shower
* "Alice in Wonderland" Tea Party

CHAPTER 3

∾

Choosing the Location

The Legion Hall or the Bride's Backyard?

Bridal showers traditionally have been held in someone's home and limited to fewer than 15 guests. Times have changed, however, and today's trendy wedding showers take place all over town, anywhere from the office conference room to a public park to a hotel banquet room. This break in tradition has occurred not only because more men are being invited to these parties but because more guests tend to be present in general. Also, party themes have become a lot more creative, requiring more interesting and unusual party sites.

Here are some things you need to consider before you select a location for your party:

The number of guests. If you're inviting less than 15 women to a bridal shower, your living room will probably be just the right size. But if you're inviting a dozen or more couples to a theme party, and especially if you'll be serving a full meal from a buffet table, you'll need a larger facility.

The time of year. Even though a patio party may seem like a good idea, if it's July in Tucson, for example, it will definitely be uncomfortably hot for the guests. But if it's a lovely spring day in Omaha, on the other hand, with temperatures in the 70s, everyone will probably have spring fever and an outdoor party may be a brilliant idea. By the way, if you expect a large crowd and there's a chance of rain, you can always extend your covered patio by renting a canopy.

Party budget. Some locations are more affordable than others. Of course, a private home is the least expensive option, but there are also affordable sites for a larger party, such as a church hall, community center, or your conference room at work.

Theme and menu. The party's theme and menu will also dictate the party's location. For instance, a Hawaiian luau requires more space than a tea party, and a formal sit-down dinner may need a rented hall, a hotel banquet room, or one of the dining rooms at your country club. A country-western barbecue would sure be more fun if it took place at a farm, on a ranch, or even in an old barn. And a garden party would be wonderful in a plush, colorful private garden, such as those found on the grounds of country estates or restored bed-and-breakfasts.

The food. Many sites require that you use their catering services, order the food and drinks on their menus, and use their wait staff, parking valets, coat attendants, bartenders, etc. If this is what you want, fine. If, however, you would like to furnish some or all of the food and the drinks yourself or would like to bring in an outside caterer, you will need to book a site that allows you to do that. Fortunately, several of the sites in the following list of popular party sites allow you to have full control, which not only means that will you save money on the site itself but that the per-person cost of the party food will be less, too.

- Private home
- Boat or houseboat
- Club meeting room
- Yacht
- Office meeting room
- Private banquet hall
- Public park
- Zoo
- Senior center
- Museum
- State or national park
- Public or private garden
- Lodge
- University
- Country club
- Church hall
- Restaurant
- Winery
- Hotel banquet room
- Beach
- Private mansion
- Elks' lodge
- Country estate
- Bed-and-breakfast
- Art gallery
- Historical society facility
- Bar facilities
- Community clubhouse

Check with your local parks and recreation department and chamber of commerce for available public and private facilities. Your local historical society can also offer you information on the most charming sites of all, especially if your theme is a family treasures shower or formal bridal tea.

Now for the hard questions...

Here are the questions you need to ask the managers of prospective sites to help you determine which site you want to book:

- How much is the rental fee?
- What is the required deposit?
- What are the fees for other services (custodial, parking, coat attendant, etc.)?

- What is available for my use (tables, chairs, utensils, coffee makers, linens, dishes, etc.)?
- Are there any restrictions (smoking, alcohol, loud music, bringing in food, drinks, or caterer)?
- Are there parking facilities?
- Is the site available for the date and time you'd most prefer to have the party?

You can use the "Party Site Information" worksheet in Chapter 14 to record the answers to these questions. Photocopy it and use one for each prospective site. In the end you'll have a basis for comparison. You'll be able to see which sites are within your budget and which ones aren't.

ೊ

CHAPTER 4

Selecting the Right Invitation

For Date and Time, See Fortune Cookie

Once you know what type of party you're going to host and where it will be held, you'll need to invite the guests. The invitations may be formal or informal, engraved or homemade, but before you go looking for the perfect invitation, let's address some basic questions.

Whom should you invite?

The traditional wedding shower has always been a party for the bride attended by her closest friends and family members, but times have changed. The trend today is toward co-ed parties that honor the bride and groom together and are attended by couples or singles who know them through church, work, school, or social activities. For most showers, however, it is still proper etiquette to invite the same people who will be guests at the wedding.

How many invitations do you need?

That depends, of course, on the number of guests who will be invited, which itself depends on the type of party you're having and where you're having it. The number of guests can vary anywhere between eight and 50. If you're hosting an elegant, all-girls tea party in your dining room, for example, you may only invite a few of the bride's closest friends and immediate family members. But if you're hosting a luau where there's plenty of room and the festive theme lends itself to a larger crowd, you may decide to invite 20 or 25 couples.

There's also the matter of money—the more guests, the more costly the party and the more invitations you'll have to buy.

What type of invitation is best?

Depending on the theme and formality of your party, an invitation may be engraved, handwritten, homemade, or even delivered by telephone, e-mail, or fax. One word of caution about telephone calls: Because most people's lives are hectic, it would probably be best to follow your phone call with something in writing so the details of the invitation won't be forgotten. If you don't, you risk having your guests forget the correct date and time or—worse yet—forget the party altogether.

An engraved or laser-printed invitation is best if the party is to be a formal occasion, such as a sit-down engagement dinner, a candlelight-and-roses dessert party, or a formal bridal tea. If the invitations are computer-generated and laser-printed, be sure to use high-quality card stock with a satin finish. Calligraphy on elegant blank note cards would also add a special touch.

An informal invitation is fine for most of the types of parties suggested in this book. You can purchase a box or two of pre-printed invitations, choosing a style that's appropriate for the theme of your party. Customize your invitations using one of those instant "personalizer machines" at the card store that prints a greeting you've made up yourself onto the cards you've selected. Or if you're a true do-it-yourselfer, here are some ideas for making invitations to match a few standard informal party themes:

Theme: Progressive Dinner.
Invitation: An invitation designed to resemble a restaurant menu, listing each course and where it will be served.

Theme: Family Treasures Shower or Far East Feast.
Invitation: A small, decorated paper fan from an import store, which unfolds to reveal the handwritten invitation, mailed in a business envelope.

Theme: Paper Shower.
Invitation: An invitation printed on a small, decorative paper plate that can be mailed in a large square envelope.

Theme: Bon Voyage!
Invitation: A "do not disturb" doorknob sign from the hotel where the party will be held or where the couple will spend their wedding night, with the invitation printed on the back (you could purchase these signs or create them yourself on a computer.) Or try writing the customized invitation out on a luggage tag attached to the travel brochure for the couple's honeymoon destination (this works well for a "home from the honeymoon" theme.)

Here are some unique themes and their corresponding invitation suggestions. Most of these invitations require hand delivery or extra postage if sent through the mail.

Theme: Christmas in July.
Invitation: Bright red Christmas balls tied with ribbons or cards announcing the party.

Theme: A Toasting.
Invitation: A scrolled invitation tucked inside a plastic or glass champagne glass.

Theme: Garden Party.
Invitation: A miniature garden trowel with a package of flower seeds and the invitation attached to the handle with a narrow ribbon.

Theme: Hawaiian Luau.
Invitation: An invitation attached to a Hawaiian lei or shell necklace that guests can wear to the party.

Theme: Country-western Barbecue.
Invitation: An invitation hanging from the rim of a miniature cowboy hat (these miniature hats can be purchased in the favors section of a party supplies store.)

Theme: Hard Hat Party.
Invitation: A child's toy hammer with the invitation attached to the handle by a narrow ribbon.

Theme: Basket Shower.
Invitation: A tiny basket with the invitation tucked inside (such baskets can also be purchased in the favors section of a party supplies store.)

Theme: Gourmet Cooking.
Invitation: A potholder with the invitation tied to its loop.

Theme: Any informal party theme.

Invitation idea #1: A cassette tape on which you have recorded an original song, poem, or limerick that incorporates the information about the party. A rap song would be fun to write for the co-ed themes. Putting new words to an old melody is another great idea. Or you can tape yourself announcing the invitation to background music that's appropriate to your theme—Hawaiian music for the luau, for example.

Invitation idea #2: Send a paperback to each guest with a homemade book jacket listing the party information (title: *A Shower for Cathy*, author: names of the hostesses, etc.).

Invitation idea #3: This one is rather puzzling—for real: Make copies of the couple's engagement photo on a color copier, using heavy-stock paper. Then photocopy the party invitation onto the back of these sheets. Cut each sheet into about 15 irregular pieces to form a jigsaw puzzle, and enclose the pieces in an envelope addressed to each guest. Of course, the guest will have to put the puzzle together in order to figure out the details of the invitation.

Tip: If you decide to have your novelty invitations delivered by hand, why not go all out and have them delivered by someone dressed to fit the theme of your party? For example, if it's an ethnic theme, have them delivered by someone dressed in an authentic costume of the culture.

What should be on the invitation?

- Name(s) of the guest(s) of honor.
- Name(s) of the host(s).
- Date and time.
- Location of the party, with map or directions if necessary. Be sure to include the telephone number of the party site in case anyone gets lost.
- Party's theme and dress code, if applicable.

- Suggested gift ideas or a list of gift registries, plus color preferences and sizes, if applicable.
- RSVP information (be sure to include a deadline).

On the next three pages are sample invitations to give you some ideas—but be as creative as your imagination allows!

When do you mail the invitations?

Formal invitations should be mailed at least four weeks ahead of time. Informal invitations may be mailed two to four weeks before the party, but if you are requesting RSVPs, allow an extra week because most people can be pretty lackadaisical about responding. In fact, you may even need to call a few people at the last minute to find out if they are coming.

A telephone invitation is appropriate whenever you're hosting a small, informal get-together of the bride's or groom's closest friends or when the party has been planned at the last minute and there isn't enough time to get invitations in the mail.

Tip: Always use the most appealing postage stamps available.

Here is an example of a formal invitation:

You are invited to attend a formal bridal tea
in honor of
Miss Estelle Marie Martin
hosted by the Misses Janice Ellsworth and Beth Edwards
Saturday, May 17 at two o'clock
1712 Helmsley Circle

Please RSVP by May 10:   *Bridal registry:*
818-7792   *Andrella's British Treasures*

Here is an example of an informal invitation:

We're Planning a Bon Voyage Party and You're Invited!

For: Our favorite couple—Bill and Ashley
When: Friday night, July 11
Time: 6 p.m.
Where: Tom and Ginny's patio
            1010 Melrose, #102
Bring: Your swimsuits and your appetites

P.S. Bring something fun for their honeymoon cruise to Acapulco!

RSVP—669-9953 or bcrane@tlg.com

And another:

❀ Aloha ❀

Grab your ukulele! Don your grass skirt!
Practice your hula!

Then join us for a luau at
Bob and Linda's grass shack (492 Penrod)
for the Big Kahuna (Ken) and his Wahini (Laura)

May 20   RSVP by May 12
6:30 pm   733-4924

CHAPTER 5

❧

Finding the Perfect Decorations

Did You Get that Idea from Martha Stewart?

When we think of party decorations, we usually think in terms of making purchases from a party supplies store or ordering a centerpiece from a florist. True, there may be some expense involved, but you'd be surprised how easy it is to use things you already have around the house. For example, you may have a beautiful old antique pitcher that can be tied with ribbons and filled with roses and greenery from your garden, or you may be able to spray-paint and decorate an old wicker laundry basket and use it to display the gifts. Now that you've read the detailed descriptions of the party themes included in Chapter 2, your head may already be swirling with ideas!

Let's begin with some of the easiest and most affordable ways to decorate.

Flowers

Whether the theme is formal or informal, flowers will create a festive spirit. You can order arrangements from your retail or supermarket florist, or you can make them yourself from any fresh or silk flowers you have available. You can also create an appearance of fullness by setting them on a mirror base.

Potted plants also work well as centerpieces, especially for a patio party or a barbecue, and you can use silk plants and ficus trees to frame your room, "dressing" them for the party with ribbons, tiny white Christmas lights, or tulle bows.

You'll also want to provide a corsage for the bride, a boutonniere for the groom, and corsages for any of the mothers or grandmothers in attendance. Whether you order the corsages from a professional florist or make them yourself, you can add novelty items that are appropriate to the shower's theme. For example, you could add measuring spoons for a gourmet cooking theme or tiny Christmas decorations for a holiday theme.

Note: If the meal is a sit-down dinner, be sure the centerpieces are low enough so the guests can see each other across the tables.

Balloons

Helium-filled balloon bouquets can be used as table centerpieces, tied to the backs of chairs or napkin rings, or set on the floor as "fillers" of color. They can also be placed at the gate or near the front door to welcome the guests as they arrive at the party. To cut down on cost, purchase your balloons in bulk from a party supplies store and rent your own helium tank. If you really want to get creative, hire a professional balloon designer to "sculpt" balloons into the shape of names, arches, or columns. You can also rig up massive balloon clusters from the ceiling.

Candles

There's nothing quite like candlelight to soften a party setting, giving it an elegant, romantic glow. Arrange floating candles, votive candles, or single candles inside hurricane lamps, surrounded by fresh or silk flowers. Or cluster a group of various lengths of long, tapered candles mounted in elegant holders.

For a food-related shower, nestle votive candles inside fruits or vegetables, such as an acorn squash or a cantaloupe (cut the fruit or vegetable in half, clean out the center, and insert the candle). For a Christmas-theme shower, insert votive candles into cored-out red apples.

Another way to use votive candles for a kitchen-theme shower is to create "kitchen grater luminaries." Wrap a dinner plate with foil and place a votive candle in the center of the plate. Cover the candle with an ordinary, metal kitchen grater, surrounded by fresh flowers or greenery. The candle's light will flicker through the slits in the grater.

Other decorative ideas

Banners. You can buy generic "Congratulations" banners from a party supplies store, or you can create personalized banners out of poster paper or by generating them on your computer.

Tiny white light strands. Generally purchased in the Christmas decoration section, these tiny white lights do wonders for a setting, creating a magical ambiance especially for an evening affair. Wind a string of lights down the center of the serving tables and around silk ficus trees and drape them over doorways or along banisters.

Tulle netting. It's inexpensive—about $1.30 per yard—so it gives you lots of bang for your buck. Swirl it down the center of your table or around the base of your centerpiece, swag it over doorways and trellises, or tie it into bows to dress up your balloon bouquets.

Crepe-paper streamers. Tastefully used, crepe-paper streamers are an affordable way to splash a little color around your party site.

Satin acetate or fabric bows. Satin acetate or fabric bows can be used as filler for floral arrangements, tied to the backs of chairs, attached to doorways or pillars, and used to embellish balloon bouquets. You can buy them or make them yourself.

Photo poster. Have a photo of the bride and groom blown up into a poster that can be displayed on an easel.

Wreaths. Decorate Styrofoam or grapevine wreaths with ribbons and miniatures that express your party's theme—for example, tiny baskets for a basket theme or sombreros and serapes for a Mexican fiesta.

"Lady's maid." A "lady's maid" is a clever decoration for a bridal shower. The maid's "body" is an ironing board. One arm is a toilet plunger and the other is a toilet bowl brush. A string mop is attached to the back of the board with the "hair" hanging over the top. Add a colander as a hat, two scouring pads as eyes, a small sponge for the nose, and a nail brush for the mouth. Tie an apron around her "waist" and tuck dish towels and potholders into the apron's pockets. You can go crazy with this if you have time, adding "jewelry," "shoes," etc. Definitely a conversation piece!

Props that can be borrowed or rented

- Tissue bells
- Foil hearts
- Antique street lamps
- Birdbaths
- Park benches
- Wishing well
- Baskets
- Stuffed animals
- Antique dolls
- Neon sign
- Parasols or umbrellas
- Tiki torches
- Patio furniture
- Miniature waterfalls
- Trellises
- Portable gazebo
- Travel posters
- Bride dolls
- Dance floor mat
- Cupids with bows and arrows
- Rafts (to fill with flowers for the pool)
- Ethnic props, Swedish horses, German beer steins, Mexican piñatas, Irish shamrocks, Chinese pagoda, etc.

Tip: Call Andersons' Party Supplies, 800-328-9640, for a catalog packed with props, invitations, and theme decorations.

Party favors

Party favors are usually set on the table for a sit-down dinner or placed in a theme-related container, such as a decorated basket for a basket shower, a sombrero for a Mexican fiesta, a Christmas stocking for a Christmas-related party, or a 10-gallon hat for a country-western theme. You get the idea!

You can purchase ready-made favors for your party or you can create your own. Here are a few creative, do-it-yourself ideas:

Miniature flower pots. These can be filled with plants or flowers and wrapped with fabric, tissue paper, or tulle netting and tied with a ribbon.

Mug with flowers. An inexpensive, colorful mug filled with flowers or a plant. Tie a bow around the handle of the mug.

Decorative fans. Decorate with lace and tie with narrow ribbons. These are appropriate for any of the bridal shower themes but especially nice for a formal bridal tea or a "family treasures" party.

"Crackers." Create these novelty favors out of crepe paper, tissue paper, and a cardboard toilet tissue tube. Wrap candies, mints, or any small novelty gift with tissue paper and stuff it inside the toilet tissue tube. Then wrap the tube longways with a piece of crepe paper (or gift wrapping paper). The paper will extend past the ends of the tube about 3" on each end. Tie each end tightly with colorful ribbon. Decorate the center of the cracker with cut-outs that coordinate with your theme. Crackers make colorful place cards if you include the guests' names on them and place them in the center of each plate.

Mini cowboy hats. Fill miniature cowboy hats with trail mix, wrap with tulle netting, and tie with a narrow ribbon. (Make your own trail mix out of chocolate chips, peanuts, and raisins.)

Soap or potpourri bags. Cut tulle netting or fabric into 7" circles or squares. Place miniature soaps or loose potpourri in the center. Gather the sides up, and tie with a ribbon. Place above each plate. To use the bags as place cards, attach a name tag to the ribbon.

Truffle boxes. Purchase gold boxes filled with two truffles each. Tie each box with a ribbon, and attach a place card. Place above each plate.

Miniature picture frames. Use a calligraphy pen and black ink to write the guests' names on parchment paper cut to fit the picture frames. Or you can computer-generate the names using a cursive or Old English font. Set the frames above the plates.

Bud vases holding a single rose. Place one rose in each bud vase. Tie with ribbon, and attach a place card.

Tiny "pots o' gold." Perfect favors for an Irish party! Cover nut cups with gold foil, and fill with several foil-covered chocolate coins.

Mini corsages or boutonnieres. Place a long-stemmed wine glass upside-down in the middle of each place setting. Place a round, white doily on top. Make simple corsages and boutonnieres out of single flowers and a sprig of baby's breath, tied together with a narrow ribbon. Place one of these on top of each doily. If you want this favor to serve as a place card, insert a corsage pin through a narrow place card and then into the center of the flowers.

Jams, jellies, or marmalade. Decorate small jars of jam, jelly, or marmalade with labels or tags with the guests' names.

Name tags

Unless you're hosting an intimate party of close friends and family members where everyone already knows each other, it's a good idea to furnish each guest with a name tag. They can be purchased from a party supplies store, or you can create your own, depending on the party's theme. For example, you can cut these simple shapes out of construction paper:

• Shamrocks for an Irish theme
• Sombreros for a Mexican fiesta

- Ships for a bon voyage party
- Christmas trees for a Christmas-related shower
- Champagne glasses for a toasting shower
- Water cans for a country garden party
- Aprons for an apron shower
- Hard hats for a hard hat shower
- Viking hats for a skandifest
- Baskets for a basket shower

Table settings

If this is a formal affair, use a linen tablecloth or a lace cloth over a solid color liner. Otherwise, you can use paper tablecloths or a theme-related, flat twin-sized sheet. For an informal buffet or an outdoor barbecue, you can wrap the napkins around sets of utensils, tie them with ribbons, and place them in a basket. Or you can roll each napkin longways (from corner to corner), and tie it around the handles of the utensils. For a more formal affair, such as a sit-down dinner or a formal bridal tea, you may want to fold the napkins into one of the many elegant designs that are so popular these days. Of course, napkin-folding is an art of its own. The more intricate patterns aren't easy to learn, but here are three of the easier folds:

The fan fold. Fold the napkin in half and, starting at one end, fold it back and forth until you have a "fan." The napkin can then be tied at the base, leaving it in the shape of a fan, tied in the center, or folded over and placed inside a long-stemmed glass.

The simple roll. Fold the napkin in half, and simply roll it up. Tie it in the center with gold braid or ribbon, with a silk or fresh flower attached.

The roll with flared top. Roll the napkin at the base, leaving the top flared out. Tie the base of the napkin with three strips of different-colored tulle netting.

Whether your party is formal or informal, it's nice to dress up your napkins with rings or ribbons. Or you can tie a flower or a favor to the center of each fan-folded napkin with a narrow ribbon.

A formal party requires glass or china plates and stemware, as well as silver or high-quality stainless utensils. An informal party allows you to use paper plates and cups and plastic utensils, but *do* buy the best-quality paper plates you can—not only sturdy to prevent mishaps, but colorful, adding to your party's theme. By the way, whether you use glass or plastic stemware, you can decorate the stems with ribbons and silk flowers.

Many of the favors listed in this chaper can also serve as place cards if you simply attach a card to the favor and place the favor in the center or at the top of each place setting. Or you can take an ordinary white place card and dress it up in one of these easy ways:

+ Write the guests' names with a silver or gold glitter pen.
+ Hot-glue a border of ruffled lace to the card.
+ Hot-glue a narrow acetate bow and tiny silk flowers to the card.
+ Punch a hole on each side of a standard white place card, and thread a rosebud horizontally through the holes.
+ Punch a hole in the upper corner of the card, and attach a tiny sleighbell with narrow red ribbon.
+ Hot-glue a border of gold or silver braid to the card.

You could also create unique "place cards" using one of these ideas:

+ Bake or buy giant sugar cookies, and write the guests' names on them in frosting, using a cake decorating kit.

- Hard-boil one egg per guest. Decorate the eggs with Easter egg dye, writing the guests' names near the top of the eggs. Display the eggs in soft-boiled-egg cups, tiny baskets filled with Easter basket grass, or homemade egg cups made from egg cartons (cut out each section and spray it gold or white).

- Using construction paper, create personalized place cards in the shape of a kite (with a colorful tail), a heart (with a ribbon tied through a hole punched in the top), a Christmas stocking (filled with tiny candy canes), a cowboy hat, or any other shape that relates to your theme.

- Paint the guests' names on wooden spoons. Tie the handles with narrow ribbon.

- Paint the guests' names on small mugs or teacups using polyester craft paint. Tie the handles with narrow ribbon.

- Use acrylic paint to write each guest's name on a refrigerator magnet cut from wood 1/8" thick by 2" long by 3" wide. Use a hot glue gun to attach a 3/4" magnet to the back of each piece of wood.

- Purchase luggage tags, or pick up a supply the next time you're at the airport, and write guests names on them.

Centerpieces

You can use a professional floral arrangement or a decorated cake for your table centerpiece, or you can use one of these clever, do-it-yourself alternatives:

Ice sculpture. If you really want to impress your guests, make your own ice sculpture by using a mold that can be purchased at most catering supply stores. There are dozens of choices, including hearts, love doves, swans, or a kissing couple.

Theme-related container. Arrange fresh or silk flowers in a theme-related container. For example:

- A wooden cricket cage for a Far East feast
- A spray-painted watering can or decorative birdcage for a country garden party
- A watermelon half for a family picnic
- A 10-gallon hat or cowboy boots for a country-western barbecue
- A German beer stein for an Oktoberfest
- A basket for a basket shower
- A hard hat or child's toy wheelbarrow for a hard hat shower
- A sombrero for a Mexican fiesta
- A chef's hat for a gourmet cooking shower

Novelty centerpieces. Depending on your theme, you can create a unique, one-of-a-kind table centerpiece with such items as:

- Antique dolls or teddy bears
- A large framed program of the evening's entertainment (amateur night)
- A spray-painted and decorated plumber's helper
- A small drawer filled with items from your own junk drawer (junk drawer shower)
- Giant wooden scissors
- "Bouquet" of kitchen utensils, such as whisks, spatulas, wooden spoons, or ladles
- A Viking ship, Swedish horses, Viking hat, or other Scandinavian souvenirs (Skandifest)
- A cuckoo clock (Oktoberfest)
- A cuckoo clock or any antique clock ("special times" shower)
- A decorated Yule log (Christmas-related shower)

- An old-fashioned balance scale
- Toy motorcycles (Harley party)
- A decorated bottle of champagne and two decorated toasting glasses
- An arrangement of parents', grandparents', and other relatives' wedding photos
- A "pot o' gold" made out of an empty half-gallon ice cream container covered with gold foil paper and filled with gold foil-wrapped chocolate coins
- A framed travel poster of Italy on a table-sized easel (Italian pasta party)
- Large round fishbowls with live goldfish
- A spray-painted and decorated Easter basket filled with Easter grass and dollar bills (paper shower)
- A miniature clothesline and clothespins to hold tiny theme-related items, such as slips and negligees (trousseau shower), towels and pillowcases (linen shower), or aprons (apron shower). These items can be cut from fabric or construction paper
- A decorated recipe box, surrounded by open cookbooks
- A decorated shower caddy ("shower shower")
- A toy boat with "Just Married" written on the side, sailing on a sea of blue cardboard waves
- A miniature hope chest made from a lined shoebox draped with lace
- Ceramic bride and groom figurines, standing on a mirror base, surrounded by flowers

Gift display

You *can* set the gifts on a table in the corner of the room, but it's much more festive to display them in a special way, drawing the guests' attention to them as they arrive. Think about your theme, and you'll come up with all kinds of ideas. Here are a few examples for inspiration:

- An enormous golf umbrella covered with satin fabric and ribbons and set on the floor to "protect" the gifts from the "elements"
- A decorated plastic or wicker laundry basket
- White picket fencing or wire fencing spray-painted gold or white surrounding the gifts in a corner of the room
- A decorated wine barrel
- A wheelbarrow draped with white lace or embroidered tablecloths and dresser scarves
- A birdbath or wishing well
- A real hope chest or an imitation made out of a cardboard box and covered with wood-grained contact paper
- A decorated Christmas tree with an attractive skirt
- A boat made from cardboard
- A box draped with Mexican serapes or Swedish table scarves

CHAPTER 6

❧

Choosing the Party Games

Let's Play...Pin the Ball-and-Chain on the Groom!

This chapter includes some of the most popular wedding shower games. As you read them over, keep several things in mind: the formality of your party, the theme of your party, and the ages of your guests. The idea is to choose games and activities that will come as close as possible to pleasing everyone.

I have divided the games into four categories:

+ Ice-breaker games
+ All-American favorites
+ Word games
+ Door prize gimmicks

Ice-breaker games

"Get acquainted" activities are great ice-breakers, especially for a "meet the family" party or any situation in which many of the guests don't know each other.

Who Am I?

This is a great ice-breaker because it forces the guests to talk to each other. Purchase a supply of 3 x 5 cards and write the name of a famous person on each. Pin one of these cards to each player's back. Each person can see the names on the backs of the other guests, but can't, of course, see his or her own. The idea of the game is for a player to determine whose name is pinned on his or her back by asking questions about that person. As the game begins, each player is allowed to ask only three yes-or-no questions per round, such as "Am I living?" or "Am I an American?" The first player to guess the name on his or her back wins a prize. By the way, be sure to have a few extra prizes on hand, just in case of a tie.

Mystery Guest Game

The host or hostess establishes a secret "mystery guest." The guests are given a list of five questions they are to ask as many guests as possible in 20 minutes, recording the answers as they go along. When the 20 minutes are up, the host describes the mystery guest and the first person who knows the mystery guest's identity wins. The idea of this game, of course, is to help the guests get acquainted with each other. You can come up with your own list of questions, but here are some examples:

- What is your hobby?
- What is your occupation?
- How many children do you have?
- How many brothers and sisters do you have?

• Where are you from originally?
• Where did you go to school?

The Memory Game

Everyone sits in a circle. The party host begins by saying (for example), "My name is Ginny, and my hobby is gardening."

Then the next person must repeat that information and add his own: "Her name is Ginny, and her hobby is gardening. My name is Jim, and my hobby is classic cars."

The third person then adds her name and hobby to the list: "Her name is Ginny, and her hobby is gardening. His name is Jim, and his hobby is classic cars. My name is Gail, and my hobby is making teddy bears." And so on.

Of course, it gets tougher and tougher the further it goes around the circle, which is why the game is so much fun. The last person who can recite everyone's name and hobby wins.

Clothespin Game

Purchase a supply of colorful plastic clothespins. Pin one clothespin on each guest's clothing, and let the game begin. Set a timer for 20 minutes. During that 20-minute period no one is allowed to say the word *no*. The idea of the game is to ask the guests questions about themselves, baiting them to answer no. Any guest who does must relinquish his clothespin to the person who tricked him or her into saying the forbidden word. When the timer rings, the guest with the most clothespins wins.

By the way, a variation of this game especially popular at bridal showers is played throughout the party. The guests are told their clothespins will be taken away by anyone who catches them crossing their legs. The guest who has caught the most women crossing their legs during the party wins.

Handwriting Analysis

Add a special "RSVP" to your invitations requesting handwriting samples from the guests to be returned to you at least two weeks in advance of the party. This gives a professional handwriting expert time to study the samples and complete an analysis of each guest's personality traits. These traits are posted on a master list under coded names. This list is then used by the guests to try to determine which guest matches which code name on the master list. The detailed handwriting analyses become party favors that are given to the guests as gifts.

All-American favorites

Charades

Charades is probably the most popular game of all. Divide the guests into two teams—evenly divided, or men against women, older generation against younger generation, etc. Each team comes up with the titles of six or eight books, movies, television shows, or songs. They write the titles on pieces of paper that are folded up and placed in a basket. The teams take turns drawing a piece of paper from the opposing team's basket, although the only person who sees the title is the person who will be acting it out.

A timer is set and this person has three minutes to silently act out the title, using his or her hands, body, and facial expressions to communicate the title to his or her team. If the timer rings before the team has guessed the title, the opposing team gets five points. If the team guesses the title before the timer goes off, they get 10 points. After each side has had six or eight turns, the team with the most points wins. In the case of a tie, play one more round. Another version of this game is to draw the clues instead of acting them out.

Note: Not everyone is comfortable "acting out" in front of a group, so it's a good idea to have fewer turns per side than team members. This means that certain team members can decline graciously without feeling pressured.

The Newlywed Game

We all know how the Newlywed Game is played. Four couples are chosen to compete. The men leave the room, and the women are asked questions, the answers to which are recorded. The men come back into the room and are asked the same questions. The object is for the men to respond with the same answers as their partners. Then, the game is reversed, and the women leave the room as the men are asked questions, and so forth. The couple with the most matching answers wins.

Here are some typical questions:
- Who is his favorite professional sports hero?
- Who is her favorite male movie star?
- When was the last time she burned the dinner?
- When was your last fight?
- What is the most embarrassing thing that ever happened to him?
- What is her most obnoxious habit?
- What turns him off about a woman?

The Observation Game

Arrange 15 or 20 items on a tray, such as a pocket knife, a pencil, a fork, and so forth. Then ask someone, such as the bride's mother, to walk slowly around the room, displaying the tray for all the guests to see.

Everyone is given paper and a pencil, and as soon as the bride's mother has left the room with the tray, the guests will be asked to write down as many things as they can remember about the *bride's mother* (color of hair and eyes, what she was wearing, etc.). The guests will moan and "cry fowl," of course, but they'll finally settle down and start recording things they remember about the bride's mother. The humor comes, of course, when the bride's mother reenters the room, and the lists are read out loud. I've seen this game played when the bride's mother was a blonde, blue-eyed woman wearing a floor-length pink skirt, but she was remembered by some guests as having "dark hair and dark eyes" and "wearing a white dress"!

The guest who has recorded the most accurate description wins a prize.

Mystery Spice

This game is usually played at bridal showers. Cover the labels on 10 different spices, such as sage, ginger, chili powder, cinnamon, nutmeg, curry powder, garlic, and thyme. Number them from "1" to "10." Furnish each guest with paper and a pencil. Pass the spices around the room, one at a time. The guests must identify the spices by sight and smell (they may not touch or taste them). The guest with the most correct answers wins.

The Liar Game

Assemble a basket of old or peculiar-looking cooking utensils and construction tools. Let each guest select one item and describe it with great eloquence—its name and purpose and a "true story" of how and when he or she used it. Those guests who recognize a certain tool or utensil will be telling the truth, but those who don't have a clue will need to fabricate their stories. Each guest is given a piece of paper and a pencil to keep track of the guests he or she thinks is lying or telling the truth. Finally, after everyone has had a turn, the person hosting the party awards prizes to the guest who had the most correct answers and to the guest who told the most creative story.

The success of this game depends on the tools and utensils, which should be so old or unusual that few, if any, of the guests will know what they are. For example, you may find a potato ricer, peach pitter, or jelly strainer hidden away in Grandma's kitchen, or a closet spud wrench, doweling jig, or bulb changer lurking in your garage.

Most Beautiful Hat Contest

Women model their hats at a bridal shower. The women, of course, come to the party wearing any kind of hat they have decorated in advance.

Apple-Peeling Contest

This is a quick little bridal shower game. Each woman is given an apple and a paring knife. The goal is to see who can make the longest continuous peel without it breaking. The longest unbroken peel wins.

The Ringer Dinger

This is a couple's contest. One person sits in a straight backed chair and holds a wooden spoon in his or her mouth with the handle sticking out. His or her partner stands about six or eight feet away and tosses 10 canning jar rings, one at a time, at the handle of the spoon, attempting to hook it. The person with the spoon can help out by maneuvering his or her head but can't get off the chair. The couple with the most ringers gets a prize.

The Communication Game

Ask three or four couples to volunteer to compete in this game. The couples compete, one couple at a time, each person sitting at a TV tray with their backs to each other so that they can't see each other's trays. One of the trays contains 15 or 20 objects that have been arranged ahead of time in a precise way. The other tray contains identical objects that are piled in a heap in the middle of the tray. The object of the game is for the person with the prearranged objects to describe the layout to his partner in such a way that his partner can duplicate it *exactly* on her tray.

You can use any small objects for this game, just so you have two of everything. For example, buttons, empty spools, chopsticks, pencils, cans of soup, paper clips, crayons of various colors, small paint brushes, forks, pieces of cord or string, children's blocks, golf balls, or tees. Once you have two of everything, the fun is in arranging the items in a complicated way—for example, with the string circling under one and over the other, or a chopstick balanced on top of the can of soup, etc. Of course, if you plan to have four couples play this game, you will need to have four trays arranged ahead of time and hidden away until game time.

Although this game is fun and challenging for the couples who compete, it is even more fun to watch, as one person tries desperately to communicate with the other. It's not as easy as it would seem! Try the game out beforehand with a partner so you'll know how it works.

Masquerade Race

This is a lot of fun for a couple's party—a competition between the men and the women. Assemble two huge shopping bags full of clothes ahead of time, one filled with men's clothes, such as pants, a belt, a long-sleeved shirt, a tie, a hat, and gloves, and the other with women's clothes, such as a *large* dress or housecoat, a belt, jewelry, a scarf, a hat, socks, and slippers.

The men "volunteer" one of their own to be "it" and the women do the same. At a given signal, the man and woman turn their backs to the guests and get dressed (over their own clothes) as fast as they can, the man donning the woman's clothes and the woman the man's. The first one completely finished wins (all zippers must be zipped; all buttons buttoned; the tie tied correctly, etc.).

Finally, they both turn around and face the guests, at which time no one cares who won, actually, because it was so much fun to watch!

Identification Game

This is another humorous couple's contest. String a couple of sheets on a clothesline across the room. Have the men stand behind the sheets exposing their bare legs and feet, from the knees down. Then have each woman try to identify her man's legs, at which time she stands in front of the sheet at that spot. Then, the sheets are removed and prizes go to those women who were right. (You'll be surprised how many women can't identify their partner's legs and feet in a game like this!)

There are several fun variations to this game. For example, you can cut holes in the sheets and have the men try to identify the women's eyes or have the women try to choose which noses belong to their partners. (This is my favorite because there's nothing quite so funny as a row of noses poking through the holes in the sheet!)

Another variation—although I don't think the men appreciate it—is for the women to identify their men's pates. The men line up behind the sheet and turn their backs so that only the tops of their heads are showing. (Nothing below the ears should be visible.)

Bridal Shower Scavenger Hunt

This actually takes place inside the women guests' purses. Set the timer for four minutes and see how many of these items each woman can find in her handbag. The guest with the most points wins.

20 points per item

$100 bill	_____	Cellular telephone	_____
Cigar	_____	Silver dollar coin	_____
Dental floss	_____	Toothbrush	_____
Dictionary	_____	Smelling salts	_____
Candy bar	_____	Magnifying glass	_____
Cotton swabs	_____	Piece of fresh fruit	_____
Alarm clock	_____	Photo of mother	_____
Pair of gloves	_____	Nail polish remover	_____
Pocket knife	_____		

10 points per item

Scissors	_____	Postage stamps	_____
Nail clippers	_____	Pencil with eraser	_____

Mascara	_____	Handkerchief	_____
Tweezers	_____	Shopping list	_____
Rubber band	_____	Breath mint/spray	_____
Calculator	_____	Zipper-top bag	_____
Face powder	_____	Eyelash curler	_____
Address book	_____	Pain reliever	_____
Notebook	_____		

5 points per item

Hair comb	_____	Lipstick/lip balm	_____
Hand lotion	_____	Nail file/emery board	_____
Tissue	_____	Regular mirror	_____
Sunglasses	_____	Photos of children	_____
Eyeglasses	_____	Chewing gum	_____
Pen	_____	Credit card	_____

TOTAL _____

Marriage Advice Poster

As the guests arrive, ask them to write a message to the engaged couple on the "marriage advice poster," which can be mounted on a decorated easel in the corner of the room. The object is for the guests to give the couple their best advice for a happy wedding, honeymoon, or married life together. Their advice can be humorous or serious.

You'll find that this poster becomes a popular attraction throughout the party as guests wander over to see who has written what. At the end of the party, a prize is awarded to the person who gave the best advice. The poster is given to the couple as a memento of the party.

Here are a few examples of advice that may be given (perhaps you can use one or two to get the poster started):

- Take time to really listen to each other. This will show you care.
- Don't ever miss a birthday, anniversary, or Valentine's Day!
- Don't wait for Christmas or a birthday—buy that special gift now.
- Get in the habit of saying, "thank you."
- Tell him you're proud of him.
- Buy romantic cards throughout the year.
- Send her flowers when it isn't her birthday.

Dress the Bride and Groom

The men take the groom into one room, and the women take the bride into another. Everyone is furnished with plenty of crepe paper, tissue paper, black, white, and colored poster paper, fabric scraps, pieces of lace and braid, and buttons, plus felt tip markers, staplers, tape, and safety pins. The men and women are given 20 minutes to "dress" the couple, fashioning a gown and veil for the bride and a suit or tuxedo for the groom. The last time I attended a shower where the bride and groom were "dressed" like this was a couples' shower given for my daughter and son-in-law. We did a pretty good job on my daughter—in fact, she *almost* looked like a real bride. Our son-in-law, however, looked pretty comical. He looked more like a giant red and green elf, complete with a pointed hat and the goofiest bowtie you've ever seen.

In any case, once the bride and groom are dressed and ready to "get married," they walk arm-in-arm "down the aisle" to the strains of everyone singing or humming "Here Comes the Bride." This is a photo opportunity you won't want to miss, so be sure to have plenty of film on hand.

Word games

The Alphabet Game

Everyone sits in a circle. Start the game by saying: "Last Saturday I had dinner at Cathy's house, and she served artichokes." The next person then repeats the sentence, adding something else to eat that begins with a "B." For example: "Last Saturday I had dinner at Cathy's house, and she served artichokes and bagels." The next person in the circle repeats this, adding an item beginning with a "C," and so forth. Any player who can't think of something to add by the count of five is out of the game. The person who stays in the game the longest wins.

The Endless Story

This is a similar game except that instead of adding a word, each guest continues a story. The person hosting usually begins a story, and after about a minute or so, she suddenly taps the shoulder of the person next to her who must pick up the story where she left off, without a break. After she has spoken for at least a minute, she taps the next person, and so on. If there is more than a moment's hesitation before the next person begins to speak, that person is out. The story continues on and on around the circle, until only a few people are left. At that point, the story-telling picks up speed until there is only one person remaining, who is declared the winner.

Tip: If it's an all-girl shower, pretend you're telling the story of a romance novel. That should make it interesting!

Word Scramble

Here is a list of words for your guests to unscramble. Make as many copies as you need. They all have to do with love and marriage. See who can unscramble the most words in three minutes. (Set a timer.)

1. **M E Y C E N R O** _____

2. **O G M O R** _____

3. **D X T O U E** _____

4. **A R O E N M C** _____

5. **S R L O P A O P** _____

6. **S B I D E R S D A M I** _____

7. **A R B D I L W N O G** _____

8. **E G A T N E G N E M** _____

9. **S R G N I** _____

10. **IBRED** _____

(Answers: ceremony; groom; tuxedo; romance; proposal; bridesmaids; bridal gown; engagement; rings; bride.)

Limerick-Writing Contest

Limericks can be a lot of fun, whether or not a party has an Irish theme. As you will see, a limerick has a certain rhythm, and once you get the hang of it, it's easy to create one tailored to the bride and groom. Basically, all you need to know is that a limerick is composed of five lines: lines one, two, and five should rhyme, and lines three and four (which are shorter) should also rhyme.

Here are a few sample limericks. Read them to your guests to get them in the mood to write their own limericks telling the couple's story. You can award prizes for the silliest, the most creative, etc.

> Here's to a sweet country miss,
> Met a guy introduced by her sis.
> They courted a year
> Until it was clear
> A marriage would bring wedded bliss.
>
> •
>
> Here's to a broker named Beau,
> Who knew how to make money grow.
> 'til a girl he found
> Made interest compound,
> And off to a wedding they'd go.
>
> •
>
> A tow-truck driver named Joe,
> Found business wherever he'd go.
> 'til the girl of his dreams
> Walked by in tight jeans—
> Now she has *him* firmly in tow.

•

They met at a cute little bistro,
In foggy San Francisco.
Until one day
He whisked her away
To the chapel in San Luis Obispo.

See how easy it is? Now you're ready to write one of your own!

Door prize gimmicks

Guests love the idea of door prizes, which may be things you've purchased and wrapped ahead of time, or part of your decorations, such as table centerpieces, potted plants, or floral arrangements. Here are a few of the most popular ways to determine who wins a door prize:

• Number the backs of the name tags before they are given to the guests as they arrive, beginning with the number "1." Then put corresponding numbers on pieces of paper, wad them up, and place them in a basket. Near the end of the party, ask the bride or groom to draw a wad of paper out of the basket. The winning number receives the prize.

• Insert three wads of paper (with predetermined numbers) inside three balloons before they are blown up with helium gas. Arrange the balloons in a bouquet as part of the decorations. Then, near the end of the party, ask the bride or groom to select one of the balloons and burst it by sitting on it (no hands allowed!). The wad of paper is then unfolded and the number read. The person with the corresponding number on the back of his name tag wins a door prize. Repeat this same procedure for the second and third balloons.

- If the party is a sit-down dinner, place a sticker under the seats of two or three of the dining room chairs. After dessert has been served, ask the guests to look under their chairs to see who has the stickers. Those who do, win prizes.
- Let the guests guess how many chocolate kisses, candy hearts, or roasted almonds there are in a large, clear glass jar. The guest who comes closest to the correct answer wins the jar full of goodies.

Suggestions for prizes

Women

- Bath powder
- Bag of potpourri
- Bracelet
- Drawer sachets
- Picture frame
- Cologne
- Decorated candle
- Bubble bath or bath salts
- Compact
- Gift basket

Men

- Humorous tie
- Money clip
- Travel kit
- Swiss army knife
- Sports trivia book
- Four-pack of cigars
- Gift certificate for a car wash
- Pen and pencil set
- Desk accessories
- Sporting goods gift certificate

Couple

- Gift certificate to a restaurant
- Two movie passes
- Bucket of gourmet popcorn
- Bottle of wine or champagne
- Two coffee mugs and a pound of coffee beans
- Basket of gourmet cheeses and crackers
- Box of candy
- Gift certificate for pizza delivery

❧

CHAPTER 7

Entertaining the Guests

And Now, a Little Song by Don Ho

In addition to the traditional party games, there are lots of other ways to entertain your guests as well. In fact, you may decide to pass on the games altogether and choose one of these popular alternatives:

"Remember when...?" slide or video show

Round up photos, slides, videos and home movies of the bride and groom, from their babyhood to the present day, and have them converted to slides or a single videotape.

Arrange them in chronological order:

1. The bride as a baby
2. The groom as a baby
3. The bride as a toddler

4. The groom as a toddler
5. The bride as a 10-year-old
6. The groom as a 10-year old
7. The bride as a junior high student
8. The groom as a junior high student

...and so forth, through their high school and college days, ending finally with their engagement photo.

We composed one of these slide shows for our daughter and son-in-law's party, using a "dissolve" feature whereby one picture gradually disappears as the next one appears, creating a continuous story. The room was darkened during this slide presentation while a friend of ours sang "Sunrise, Sunset" and played guitar. There were many "oohs" and "aahs" and everyone really seemed to enjoy it, including the bride and groom. (It's a good thing the room was dark, because I dribbled with tears all the way through it!)

Karaoke

Rent a karaoke machine (consult "Disk jockeys" in your local yellow page listings), and you'll have all the entertainment you can handle for an evening! Usually one or two guests will have sung to a karaoke machine before, and with just a little encouragement, they'll be glad to "demonstrate" how the concept works. The next thing you know, they're really enjoying themselves, which will encourage the rest of your guests to give it a try.

DJ or live band

If your party theme lends itself to dancing—such as a country-western barbecue, a formal engagement dinner, or one of the ethnic parties—you may want to hire a band or a DJ.

Jukebox

Guests seem to get a kick out of an old-fashioned jukebox, not only because of the novelty of it, but because they can select their own music. This is a great idea for any informal party. (To find a jukebox you can rent, look under "Disk jockeys," "Entertainment," or "Party rentals" in your local yellow pages.)

Instrumentalists or vocalists

If you're hosting a formal party, you may decide to engage the services of professional musicians to perform during the meal, such as a stringed trio, a harpist, or a pianist, or if you really want to impress your guests as they enjoy their after-dinner coffee, arrange for a soloist or instrumentalist to present a mini concert.

Ethnic parties call for special music, as well. For example, you may want to hire mariachi singers for your Mexican fiesta or strolling violinists for your Italian pasta party.

Christmas caroling or a sing-along

Certain party themes lend themselves to group singing, such as a Christmas-related party, Irish-theme party, or any of the other ethnic parties. If you decide to include caroling or a sing-along as part of your entertainment, be sure to furnish song sheets for each of the guests. (I'm always amazed at how few carols we *really* know by heart, especially when it comes to the second and third verses!)

Barbershop quartet

Call your local chamber of commerce for the name and number of your local barbershop singing club. These men love to entertain and are always looking for ways to keep barbershop music alive.

Background music

If nothing else, be sure to provide soft background music. It should be just loud enough to enhance the party's ambiance but not so loud that the guests have difficulty with conversation.

"The Wedding Night"

This is a very simple but deliciously devious idea whereby someone discreetly writes down the exact words of the bride and/or groom as they open their gifts. Then, after all the gifts have been opened, these words and phrases are read out loud as the supposed "dialogue" of the bride and groom on their wedding night. This brings a lot of laughs because most of the comments can be taken with a double meaning. For example: "...I can't wait to unwrap this...It looks pretty interesting... Oh...My...It's wonderful...just what I was hoping for...Wow! ...Oh, I love it...It's just great...Thank you...How did you know this is what I needed?...I'll use this every morning as soon as I wake up..."

See how it works? What fun!

Specialty entertainment

Depending on your party's theme, you may want to consider some of these options:

- Polynesian dancers and performers (torch or knife juggling, etc.)
- Folk dancers (great for any of the ethnic parties)
- "Glamour makeovers" by your favorite cosmetic line rep
- Synchronized swimming performance (appropriate for a poolside party)
- Caricaturist (everyone gets a kick out of seeing their appearance in the eyes of a caricaturist)
- Horse and carriage rides

- Hay wagon rides
- Hot-air balloon rides
- Hula lessons
- Mime performance
- Magic show
- Juggling act
- Clown act
- Balloon artist show
- Stand-up comedy routine
- A recorded message for the bride and/or groom (on cassette or videotape) from close friends or family members who weren't able to attend the party
- An amateur photographer taking instant photos of the guests—group shots, as well as individual photos of each guest standing beside the bride or groom. As these photos "develop," pass them around for everyone to see, then place them in an album to be given to the bride or groom as a memento of the party.
- Amateur videographer videotaping the party, beginning with the exterior and interior decorations before the guests have arrived and continuing with the games, activities, gift opening, etc. Also, let your guests know in advance that they will be asked to "say a little something to the couple" on the tape. The tape is then given to the bride or groom as a gift.

A "roasting"

Although this usually follows a sit-down dinner, as described in detail in Chapter 2, it can be the main entertainment for any type of party. The point of a "roasting," of course, is to take turns telling embarrassing little stories about the bride or groom, but only in fun—never revealing anything too personal or humiliating. For example, the bride's best friend might tell about the time the bride unknowingly stepped in a "doggie gift" on her way to speak at a women's luncheon and how the stench permeated the room throughout her speech. Or the groom's dad might tell about the time he was teaching his son to drive and some of the klutzy things his son did. A successful roasting depends on how well you've done your research and how well-prepared the guests are to tell their *harmless* stories.

CHAPTER 8

☙

A Collection of Engagement Toasts

To the Lovely Bride: May You Always Wear the Pants

One of the host's duties is to toast the happy couple. You can compose an original toast from your heart, or you may choose one of the sample toasts that follow. I have placed them in four categories: traditional, contemporary, classic, and ethnic.

Traditional toasts

"Ladies and gentlemen, please stand with me as we raise our glasses in a toast to _____ and _____. Congratulations on your engagement. We wish you a lifetime of health and happiness."

◆

"I feel honored to have been asked to give the traditional toast to the bride and groom on this momentous occasion. _____ and _____, may your lives be filled with joy, good health, and a lifetime of happiness."

◆

"Ladies and gentlemen, it is now my pleasure to propose a toast to our newly engaged couple. To love, which is nothing unless it's divided by two."

◆

"It is now my honor to toast _____ and _____, two very nice people. I wish you good health, happiness, and a wonderful life together. Congratulations on your engagement to be married."

◆

"_____ and _____, may the road you now travel together be filled with much love and success. Congratulations to you both."

Contemporary toasts

"To fate, which brought you together, and to love, which will keep you happy forever. Congratulations, and God bless."

◆

"_____ and _____, it is an honor to toast to your engagement. May this be the start of something wonderful, a brand-new life, a beautiful beginning. Here's to a future filled with romance, delight, sharing, laughter, and great adventure, as your love grows with each day."

◆

"To a couple destined for a world of success, not only in life, but in love. Congratulations, my friends!"

◆

"I would like to propose a toast to our lovely couple. May the joy of your love grow deeper with each hour, may your friendship grow closer each day, and may your marriage grow richer each and every year. I love you both. Congratulations, and cheers!"

◆

"No sooner met, but they looked;
    No sooner looked but they loved;
No sooner loved but they sighed;
    No sooner sighed but they asked one another the reason;
No sooner knew the reason but they sought the remedy."
These are the words of Shakespeare, but aren't they true of _____ and _____, for "no sooner looked but they loved." May we call it "love at first sight"? I think so. We all raise our glasses in a toast to you, _____ and _____, as we celebrate your engagement. Congratulations!"

◆

"Please stand with me as we honor _____ and _____ with a toast. We wish you joy of heart, peace of mind, and the beautiful blessing of love. Congratulations!"

◆

"_____ and _____, life is so much better when it's shared, and I'm so glad you found each other. May your days be bright and happy because of the very special joys that come with living...giving...caring. Congratulations on your engagement!"

◆

"It has occurred to me that certain people just seem destined to find each other, and I know that everyone in this room realizes this is true of _____ and _____. Not only do they understand and believe in each other, but they fill each other's needs and support each other's dreams. As a matter of fact, every little nook and cranny of their lives seem to fit together perfectly. To two lucky people who found each other in time. Congratulations!"

◆

"Ladies and gentlemen, it is a pleasure to propose a toast to our newly engaged couple. I wish for you three things: warm moments shared together; thousands of tomorrows bright with love; and a lifetime of dreams come true. Cheers and congratulations!"

Classic toasts

"It is my privilege and honor to propose this toast to the happy couple. John Keats said, 'A thing of beauty is a joy forever; its loveliness increases; it will never pass into nothingness.'

"My wish for you, _____ and _____, is that your marriage will be a thing of beauty and a joy forever. And may the loveliness of your union increase with each year."

◆

"Martin Luther said, 'There is no more lovely, friendly, and charming relationship, communion, or company than a good marriage.' Here's to _____ and_____. Congratulations on your engagement and may your married life be a charming relationship and a lovely communion of spirits."

◆

"_____ and _____, Shakespeare wrote, 'Love cometh like sunshine after rain.' We're all so happy that you have found each other. Congratulations on your engagement."

◆

"Look down you gods, and on this couple drop a blessed crown."

—Shakespeare

Ethnic toasts

Australian—"Cheers!"

Austrian—"Prosit!" (May it be to your health!)

Brazilian—"Saude!" (To your health!)

British—"I give you a toast. May you always be two out and one in: out of debt, out of danger—and in good health!"

Canadian—"Cheerio! Good times!"

Chinese—"Kan pei!" (Bottoms up!)

Dutch—"Op je gezondheid!" (To your health!)

French—"A votre sante, bonheur, et prosperite!" (To your health, happiness, and wealth!)

German—"Ofen warm, Bier kalt, Weib jung, Wein alt." (Oven warm, beer cold, wife young, wine old.)

Greek—"Stin ygia sou!" (To your health!)

Gypsy—"May you live until a dead horse kicks you!"

Hawaiian—"Hauoli maoli oe!" (To your happiness!)

Irish—"May you have warm words on a cold evening,
A full moon on a dark night.

May the roof above you never fall in,
   And the friends gathered below never fall out.
May you never be in want,
   And always have a soft pillow for your head.
May you be 40 years in heaven,
   Before the devil knows you're dead.
May you be poor in misfortunes, rich in blessings,
   Slow to make enemies and quick to make friends.
But be you rich or poor, quick or slow,
   May you know nothing but happiness from this
   day forward."

(A combination of several traditional Irish toasts.)

Italian—"Viva l'amor!" (Long live love!)

Japanese—"Konotabi wa omedeto gozaimasu."
(Congratulations to the bride and groom.)

Jewish—"Mazel tov!" (Congratulations!)

Mexican—"Salud y tu amor!" (To your health and to your love!)

Polish—"Na zdrowie i dtugie zycie!" (To your health and long life!)

Portuguese—"A sua felicidade!" (To your happiness!)

Russian—"Za Zdorovie molodech!" (To the health of the young couple!)

Scandinavian—"Skal!" (Your health!)

Scottish—"May the best ye've ever seen
         Be the worst ye'll ever see,
       May a mouse ne'er leave yer girnal
         Wi a tear drap in his 'ee,
       May ye aye keep hale and he'rty
         Till yere auld enough tae dee,
       May ye aye be juist as happy
         As I wish ye aye tae be."

Spanish—"Salud, pesetas y amor...Y tiempo para gozar-los!" (Health, money and love...And time to enjoy them!)

Thai—"Chai yo!" (To your health and well-being!)

Welsh—"Eiechid da, a whye fahr!" (Good health and lots of fun!)

Note: You may want to pick up a copy of my book, *Complete Book of Wedding Toasts*, which includes hundreds more ready-to-use toasts.

❧PART II❧

Preparing the
Spread

You probably have dozens of your own tried-and-true party recipes, but in case you're looking for some fresh ideas, the next four chapters contain recipes your guests will love. Although the menus are divided into three main categories—informal, formal, and international—they can be mixed and matched at will or used to supplement your own creations.

You'll notice that many of the recipes are marked with an asterisk (*), which means they are relatively low in fat and calories. When estimating how much food to prepare for your guests, it's a good idea to plan on the high side. If you have a lot of food left over, your family will appreciate the treats, and you won't need to cook again for a few days.

By the way, if you plan to serve your food from a buffet, give your table a professional look by elevating the food dishes and adding colorful touches between the dishes and on the serving trays. Huge strawberries are always a good idea, as well as melon slices, parsley, ribbons, greenery, or fresh flowers. Also, mirrors beneath the platters make the food appear more plentiful.

Have fun as you plan your party menu!

CHAPTER 9

꙳

Informal Cuisine

This chapter contains menus for every type of informal party. I've divided them into these categories:
- Snacks and appetizers
- Luncheon buffet
- Barbecue bash
- Breakfast buffet
- Hawaiian luau
- Desserts

These recipes have already been "party-tested" and are sure to please!

Snacks and appetizers

Snacks and appetizers can be made to look more abundant by serving them on the largest trays you can find. Even an aluminum pizza tray will do. The key to an attractive presentation, however, is to cover the trays first with paper doilies. In fact, you'll be amazed to see how doilies can be used to dress up the simplest of snacks.

Here are several recipes for party snacks and appetizers for you to consider:

Apricot Nut Surprise

1 pound dried apricots
1 tablespoon finely chopped nuts
1 teaspoon lemon juice

3 ounces softened cream cheese
2 tablespoons lemon-flavored yogurt
1 tablespoon confectioners' sugar

Whip together the cream cheese, yogurt, lemon juice, and confectioners' sugar. Fold in the chopped nuts. Use a sharp knife to cut a pocket in each apricot. Fill each apricot with 1 teaspoon of the filling. Refrigerate for at least an hour and sprinkle with confectioners' sugar before serving. (Makes 60 servings.)

Jalapeño Pinto Pinwheels*

1 8-ounce package cream cheese
1/3 cup finely chopped red onion
2 finely chopped jalepeño peppers
1/8 teaspoon garlic power
1/2 cup chopped black olives
1 small bottle chunky salsa

1 cup shredded Monterey jack cheese
1 cup sour cream
1/2 teaspoon seasoned salt
1 15-ounce can pinto beans, drained
1/4 cup chopped pimientos
5 large flour tortillas

Blend everything together except the beans and tortillas. Cover and refrigerate for at least 3 hours. Whip beans in a food processor until smooth. Spread each tortilla with a thin layer of beans and cover with a thin layer of the refrigerated mixture. Roll up the tortillas tightly, wrap in foil, and refrigerate for 1 hour. Cut into 1-inch slices and serve "pinwheel" side up on plate garnished with salsa. (Makes 15 servings.)

Parmesan Mushrooms*

3 pounds large fresh mushrooms

3/4 cup finely chopped green onions

1/2 cup no-fat mayonnaise

1 teaspoon garlic power

1 tablespoon red wine

6 tablespoons extra virgin olive oil

2 cups finely chopped red bell pepper

1/4 cup Dijon mustard

1 teaspoon dried oregano

4 tablespoons grated Parmesan cheese

Remove mushroom stems. Roll mushrooms in oil and broil (caps right side up) for 6 to 8 minutes until tender. Chop the mushroom stems and add to the onions and bell pepper; sauté in oil for 4 minutes. Add wine and sauté for another minute. Add the mayonnaise and mustard. Stir mixture well, and spoon 1 teasponful into each mushroom cap. Sprinkle with the Parmesan cheese and broil until brown. (Makes 12 servings.)

Party Gorp

Peanuts

M&Ms

Chopped dates

Crumbled Heath bars

Raisins

Sunflower seeds

Chocolate chips

If you want an irresistible snack that's easy to prepare, mix these ingredients together and serve in bowls or baskets.

Snack Mix

1 box Wheat Chex

1 box Corn Chex

1 large jar peanuts

1 pound butter

1 tablespoon onion salt

1 box Rice Chex

1 large can mixed nuts

1 package thin pretzels

2 tablespoons chili powder

1/4 cup Worcestershire sauce

Pour the cereals, nuts, and pretzels into a flat metal baking pan. Melt butter and seasonings together over low heat. Pour over the cereal/nut mixture and bake in 250-degree oven for 45 minutes. Serve when cooled.

Dips

Along with any kind of sturdy chips, serve 1 or more of these homemade dips:

Guacamole

4 ripe avocados
1 carton (16 ounces) low-fat cottage cheese
1/4 cup lemon juice
2 teaspoons chili powder
8 sliced black olives
3/4 cup chopped green onions
1/2 cup drained jalapeño pepper slices
2 cloves garlic
1/2 cup chopped tomato
1 jar salsa

Put aside half of the onions, plus the chopped tomatoes, olives, and salsa; blend the rest in a blender or food processor until smooth, adding salsa until the mixture is soft enough to be dipped without breaking the chips. Scoop the mixture into a bowl and garnish with remaining onions, tomatoes and olives. (Makes 12 servings.)

Horseradish Crab Dip*

2 1/2 cups imitation crab meat, shredded
3 8-ounce packages light Neufchatel cream cheese, softened
1 1/2 cups undiluted evaporated skimmed milk
1/2 cup finely sliced green onions
1/2 cup finely chopped red bell pepper
1 teaspoon garlic salt
2 teaspoons prepared horseradish

Whip the milk and cream cheese together; stir in the rest of the ingredients. Cover and refrigerate for 2 hours. (Makes 6 cups.)

Creamy Spinach Dip in a Bread Bowl *
3 large round sourdough loaves of French bread
4 cups low-fat yogurt
2 10-ounce packages of frozen chopped spinach, thawed and
squeezed dry
1/2 cup reduced-calorie mayonnaise
2 packages dry onion soup mix

Mix together the yogurt, spinach, mayonnaise, and onion soup
mix; cover and chill in the refrigerator for up to 4 hours. Use a
sharp knife to hollow out the loaves of French bread. Fill the
bread "bowls" with the spinach mixture, and serve with the
scooped-out bread pieces, which can be used as "dippers."
(Makes 20 servings.)

Cilantro Bean Dip*
2 cans drained black beans
1 cup low-fat sour cream
1/4 cup chopped cilantro
2 teaspoons chili powder
2 teaspoons hot sauce

1 cup nonfat mayonnaise
2 cans chopped green chilies,
drained
1 teaspoon garlic powder

Mash beans with a fork or with food processor on slow speed.
Mix in remaining ingredients, cover and refrigerate for 1 hour.
(Makes 5 cups.)

Clam Cocktail Dip*
4 cups low-fat sour cream
3 6 1/4 ounce cans minced clams, drained
1/2 cup chopped green onions (put aside half)
1/4 cup Worcestershire sauce
1/2 teaspoon black pepper

Mix the ingredients together and chill in the refrigerator for at
least 2 hours. Serve in a brightly colored bowl. Add remaining
onions as garnish. (Makes approximately 4 cups.)

Easy Appetizers
- **Strawberry Ring.*** Arrange large fresh strawberries in a ring around a bowl of confectioners' sugar for dipping.
- **Shrimp Cocktail.** Arrange large cooked shrimp in a ring around a bowl of cocktail sauce.
- **Oysters on the Half-Shell.** Wash oysters in shells. Chill. Open. Arrange halves on a plate of crushed ice, in a ring around a bowl of cocktail sauce.
- **Broiled Cocktail Sausages.** Cut a cabbage into 2 halves and place cut-side down on 2 plates. Broil cocktail sausages. Skewer them with long wooden or plastic party picks, and stick them into the cabbages, capping each pick with a black olive.
- **Ham-and-Cream-Cheese Rolls.** Spread thin ham slices with pineapple-cream cheese. Roll and skewer with short plastic party picks.

Note: You may also want to consider serving Mexican Nachos or Swedish Meatballs, described in Chapter 11.

Breakfast buffet

A note regarding buffets, breakfast or otherwise: The latest trend is to serve food from several food stations as opposed to one buffet table. For a breakfast buffet, for example, this would mean that your hot dishes would be served from one station, your pastries and fruit from another, and your drinks from yet another. Guests seem to prefer this arrangement because they can "get at the food" faster, and hosts like it better because it makes the food look more plentiful.

Basic Breakfast
- Bacon, ham, or sausage
- Hot buttered biscuits
- Scrambled eggs
- Warm pastries

- Orange juice
- Coffee and tea
- Bowl of fresh berries

Pancake or Waffle Breakfast

- Bacon, ham, or sausage
- Hot maple syrup
- Boysenberry syrup
- Bowl of fresh berries
- Pancakes or waffles
- Blueberry syrup
- Orange juice
- Coffee and tea

Note: For a more formal breakfast, see Champagne Breakfast, Chapter 10.

Luncheon buffet

Providing simple but delicious finger foods is a wise way to pare down the fuss and planning, so you can keep the focus on the fun and festivities. Just prepare these trays—stationed in numerous locations—and let your guests graze!

Antipasto Tray*

8 ounces of sliced oven-roasted turkey breast
1 large can jumbo pitted black olives, drained
1 8-ounce package sliced salami
1 8-ounce package sliced prosciutto
8 ounces provolone cheese slices
8 ounces of jalapeño Monterey jack cheese, cut into 1-inch cubes
6-ounce jar of pimiento-stuffed green olives, drained
Deviled eggs topped with anchovies
Marinated mushrooms
Cherry tomatoes, radishes, and scallions
Celery stuffed with chicken salad, cream cheese, deviled ham, or prepared cheese spreads
1 7-ounce jar of cobs of baby corn, drained
3 6-ounce jars of marinated artichoke hearts, drained
Breadsticks

Place a glass or mug in the middle of a large circular tray, and fill it with the breadsticks. Arrange the rest of the ingredients on the tray and serve. (Makes 24 servings.)

Party Sandwich Potpourri
40 slices of party rye
40 small endive or butter lettuce leaves
1 large can tuna, drained and flaked
1/2 pound frozen cooked bay shrimp, thawed
1/2 medium cucumber, thinly sliced
1 cup nonfat mayonnaise
1/4 cup Dijon mustard
And a few of the following:

Pimiento strips	Caviar
Sliced green onion	Small tomato slices
Steamed frozen peapods	Steamed fresh asparagus tips
Dill sprigs	Jumbo, pitted black olives, sliced in half

Lay out the bread and crackers and begin "decorating" with the ingredients listed above. First, moisten them with mayonnaise and/or mustard, and then lay 2 or 3 ingredients on each, being as creative as possible so that each one looks like a different "work of art." To show them off, arrange them on the darkest tray you can find—preferably black. (Makes 40 servings.)

Fresh Fruit Tray*
Any fresh fruit will work, although strawberries, melons, and grapes are popular choices because they hold up well and have a showy appearance.

Sunshine Slaw
4 cups shredded cabbage
1 large can sliced peaches, drained
1 cup chopped celery
1/2 cup chopped bell pepper
1 1/2 cups miniature marshmallows
Enough mayonnaise to moisten

Combine ingredients, mix well and chill. (Makes 10 servings.)

Sweet Waldorf Salad

4 cups diced red delicious apples
1 teaspoon lemon juice
Dash of salt
1 cup whipped cream

2 tablespoons sugar
2 cups diced celery
2 cups walnut pieces
1/2 cup mayonnaise

Mix together the mayonnaise, sugar, lemon juice, salt, and whipped cream. Add apples, celery, and walnuts, and chill. (Makes 12 servings.)

Tomato Flower Potato Salad

12 extra-large chilled tomatoes
12 medium potatoes
1/2 cup finely chopped red onions
1 cup chopped celery
4 hardboiled eggs, cut up
1 head red leaf lettuce

2 teaspoons salt
1/2 teaspoon pepper
1/2 cup Italian salad dressing
1 cup mayonnaise
2 tablespoons mustard
1 small can sliced ripe olives

Boil potatoes in salted water until tender. Drain, cool, and peel. Cut potatoes into small cubes. Combine with onion, celery, and eggs. Combine salad dressing, mayonnaise, mustard, salt and pepper, and add to potato mixture. Cover and refrigerate for 3 to 4 hours. Cut off stem ends of chilled tomatoes to give them flat bottoms for stability. With cut side down, cut each tomato into sixths, cutting down to within a 1/2-inch of the bottom. *Carefully* spread the sections apart, forming a "flower." Fill tomatoes with chilled potato mixture, top with olives, and serve on large platter lined with red leaf lettuce.

Tossed Green Salad*

Tear your favorite lettuce into bite-size pieces, and combine with sliced tomatoes, green onions, artichoke hearts, fresh sliced mushrooms, canned garbanzo beans, and slices of avocado. Serve with a variety of dressings on the side.

Note: Several of the snack and appetizer ideas mentioned earlier may also be added to your luncheon buffet, such as the Apricot Nut Surprise or Jalapeño Pinto Pinwheels. Many of the international dishes included in Chapter 11 will also work, whether or not your party has an ethnic theme.

Hawaiian luau

As I was researching for this book, I found the luau to be the most popular party theme of all. I don't know if it reminds the guests of their carefree Hawaiian vacations or if it just seems like a festive, "hang-loose" kind of party. A creative food display will also add to the party's ambiance. By the way, a luau is one of those meals that *should* be served from one table.

Here are a few of the items usually served at a luau:

- Roast pork
- Grilled fish
- Fresh pineapple slices, soaked in teriyaki sauce and lightly grilled
- Fresh strawberries
- Melons
- Papayas
- Sweet Hawaiian bread
- Boiled sweet potatoes
- Roasted bananas (peel, dip in melted butter, and sprinkle with sugar; wrap in aluminum foil and roast for 20 minutes; serve with a drizzle of rum)

- Bowls of sweet, fresh coconut
- Fresh green salad with tomatoes, onions, raw zucchini squash, cucumbers and plenty of ripe avocados
- Hawaiian fruit salad (see the recipe following this list)
- Bowls of macadamia nuts
- And, of course, a bowl of poi, that stuff everyone says tastes like wallpaper paste. (I think it tastes like "nothing," and yet it's a "must" for any luau, as a conversation piece if nothing else!)

Tip: If you would like to cook a whole pig in an authentic Hawaiian earth oven, the detailed directions for making the oven and cooking the pig can be found in The Hawaiian Luau Book, *by Lee and Mae Keao.*

Hawaiian Fruit Salad
1 cup sour cream
1 cup shredded coconut
1 cup pineapple tidbits, drained
1-1/2 cups mandarin oranges, drained
1-1/2 cups miniature marshmallows
Freshly ground nutmeg

Combine all ingredients except nutmeg, and let chill in the refrigerator overnight. Sprinkle with nutmeg just before serving.

Barbecue bash

In addition to the usual hot dogs, hamburgers, steaks, chicken or turkey fillets, here are a few interesting alternatives:

Steak Kabobs
3 pounds lean round steak
3 green bell peppers
4 cloves garlic
2 teaspoons cornstarch
3 red bell peppers
1-1/2 cups steak sauce
2 cups beer
2 teaspoons ground cumin

Crush the garlic and add it to the beer, cornstarch and cumin; stir well. Cut the round steak into 3/4-inch strips, place in a glass bowl, and cover with the garlic-beer marinade. Refrigerate for 3 to 4 hours. Remove steak from the marinade (save the marinade). Cut the bell peppers into 2-inch pieces. Thread the steak and pepper pieces alternately onto 12 skewers (leave space between each piece). Place the remaining marinade in a pan, add the cornstarch, and bring to a boil. Place the kabobs on the grill and cook for approximately 15 minutes, turning and brushing with marinade frequently. (Makes 12 servings.)

Turkey-Ginger Root Kabobs*

3 medium zucchini squash	3 large red bell peppers
1 cup red wine vinegar	2/3 cup corn syrup
1/4 cup soy sauce	2 tablespoons grated ginger root
3/4 teaspoon garlic powder	3/4 teaspoon pepper
1-1/2 pounds turkey breast tenderloin steaks	

Combine vinegar, corn syrup, soy sauce, ginger root, garlic powder, and pepper for marinade. Rinse turkey and pat dry; cut lengthwise into 1-inch strips. Soak in marinade for 1 hour in the refrigerator. Cut zucchini and red peppers into 1-inch pieces and thread onto 12 skewers, alternating with turkey strips (leave space between each piece). Place on grill for 10 to 12 minutes, marinating frequently. (Makes 12 servings.)

Grilled Corn on the Cob*

Soak the corn (husk and all) under water for about 15 minutes. Then lay the corn, still in its husks, over the coals for about 20 minutes, turning *constantly*.

Grilled Red Potatoes*

Split potatoes, sprinkle with garlic salt, and spray with buttered-flavored oil. Wrap in heavy-duty foil and place over hottest coals for about 30 minutes.

Desserts

In place of—or in addition to—a traditional decorated cake from the bakery, here are four more party favorites:

Heavenly Blueberry Surprise*
It's hard to believe that a serving of anything this delicious only has 135 calories and 2 grams of fat—but it's true!

1/2 gallon of nonfat vanilla ice cream or frozen yogurt
3 small cantaloupes, thinly sliced and peeled
3 cups fresh or frozen blueberries (or you can use raspberries or
  strawberries)
2-1/2 cups orange juice
2-1/4 tablespoons cornstarch
2/3 cup sugar

In a small saucepan stir together the sugar and cornstarch. Add the orange juice and berries. Cook and stir until it begins to thicken, then cook for 2 more minutes. Cool in refrigerator for 20 minutes. Scoop 1/3 cup of ice cream or yogurt into each dessert dish. Arrange cantaloupe slices on one side of the dish. Pour berry sauce over top of ice cream or yogurt. Serve immediately. (Makes 20 servings.)

Melon Ball Compotes*
1/2 gallon raspberry sherbet
10 cups melon balls
3 cups chilled ginger ale

For each serving, surround 1 scoop of sherbet with 6 or 8 small melon balls. Pour 1/4 cup ginger ale over the top. (Makes 12 servings.)

Death by Chocolate

This *definitely* has more than 135 calories and 2 grams of fat! But what the heck!

2 19.8-ounce boxes fudge brownie mix
1 cup Kahlua
16 Heath candy bars
2 12-ounce containers whipped topping

Bake the brownies according to directions and cool. Punch holes in brownies with a fork and pour the Kahlua over the top. Tap the Heath bars with a hammer while still in the wrapper, and crumble the pieces over the top of the soaked brownies. Top with whipped topping. (Don't worry—you'll probably only gain 3 or 4 pounds!)

Do-It-Yourself Sundaes

Serve bowls of various flavors of ice cream. Then let the guests make their own sundaes by adding any of the following:

Sauces:
- Chocolate sauce
- Hot fudge sauce
- Butterscotch sauce
- Caramel sauce
- Kiwi sauce (blend 3 peeled kiwi, 3 tablespoons honey, 2 teaspoons lemon juice, 1 teaspoon vanilla)

Fruits:
- Strawberries
- Raspberries
- Boysenberries
- Sliced bananas
- Sliced mango
- Sliced kiwi
- Sliced peaches

Nuts:
- Chopped walnuts
- Chopped pecans
- Chopped almonds
- Chopped peanuts

Crumbled candy bars:
- Heath Bars
- Butterfingers
- Hershey Bars

Whipped toppings:
- Cool Whip
- Freshly whipped cream

Note: You may also want to consider these desserts, which are included in the next two chapters: Swedish Macaroon Tea Cakes, Irish Appleberry Crunch, Mexican Sopaipilla, and Berry Trifle, plus the Festive Dessert Drinks in Chapter 11, such as the Cappuccino Float.

Tip: For a dramatic flair, turn the lights down low and enter the room carrying dessert topped with lighted sparklers!

CHAPTER 10

❧

Formal Cuisine

This chapter contains three elegant menus that are suitable for formal parties:
- Champagne breakfast
- An elegant tea party
- Formal sit-down dinner

Champagne breakfast

A champagne breakfast is more formal than either of the two breakfast buffets described in the last chapter. It will require your finest linen tablecloth and napkins, china, crystal and silver service, champagne flutes, and a silver wine cooler, if possible. The following is an elegant menu to provide:
- Chilled tomato and orange juice
- Canadian bacon
- Scrambled eggs with sauteed mushrooms and green onions (add one tablespoon of cream per egg)
- Large fresh strawberries with fresh whipped cream

- Thinly sliced nut, banana, orange, and raisin breads, with butter and cream cheese
- Hot croissant rolls with berry preserves
- Regular coffee, specialty coffees (see Chapter 11) and, of course, chilled champagne

An elegant tea party

The tea. The secret to an excellent cup of tea is to start with cold water, which you bring to a roaring boil. Meanwhile, pre-warm the teapot by filling it with hot water from the tap. It is impractical to repeat this process continually if you have a large group, so keep a large carafe of hot water available.

There are all kinds of tea: herbal, black, spiced, orange pekoe and, of course, hundreds of scented and blended teas, each with their own exotic brand names. Flavored liqueurs may also be added. As hostess, you may serve any tea of your choice.

Tea sandwiches. These sandwiches differ from the party sandwiches described in the previous chapter in that they are smaller, fancier and more time-consuming to put together. Start with thinly sliced breads, such as rye, pumpernickel or any of the "diet breads" on the market. Instead of mayonnaise and mustard, these delicate finger sandwiches start with softened butter, which will keep the fillings from making the bread soggy.

1. Cover each piece of bread with butter.
2. Make the sandwiches whole, wrap, and refrigerate.
3. Shortly before serving, remove from the refrigerator, trim off the crusts and cut into shapes: rectangles; triangles; squares; rounds, hearts, and any other fancy shape that can be cut with a cookie cutter. (The bread cuts cleanly when cold.)

Here are some of the most popular fillings, but remember to always butter the bread first, regardless of what other garnishes may be added:

- **Ham and Swiss.** Thinly sliced ham and Swiss cheese slices, garnished with Dijon mustard.
- **Turkey and cranberry.** Thinly sliced turkey, garnished with a mixture of whole cranberry sauce and Dijon mustard.
- **Salmon and cream cheese.** A layer of softened cream cheese (thinned with cream and fresh dill) and a thin layer of smoked salmon.
- **Egg and black olive.** A filling made from 8 hard-boiled eggs that have been crumbled and mixed with 1/4 cup mayonnaise, 1/4 cup plain yogurt, 3 teaspoons curry power and 1 small can of chopped black olives.
- **Walnuts and cream cheese.** A mixture of one package softened cream cheese, whipped until smooth with 1/4 cup cream. Then add 1/2 cup finely-diced celery and 1/2 cup chopped almonds or walnuts.
- **Pineapple and cream cheese.** A mixture of 1 package softened cream cheese, whipped until smooth with 1/4 cup cream. Then add 1 cup well-drained crushed pineapple. (This is my personal favorite, especially when served on Boston brown bread.)
- **Chicken and bacon.** Whip butter with a splash of lemon juice, 1/2 teaspoon of Dijon mustard and 1 tablespoon of mayonnaise. Mix with chopped chicken breast and finely crumbled bacon.
- **Apricot and cream cheese.** Mix 1 cup of apricot preserves with one cup softened cream cheese and spread on the bread. Add thinly sliced ham.

• **Cucumber and watercress.*** Now here's something really British! Alternate layers of thinly sliced cucumbers (sprinkled with vinegar and salt) and watercress.

Scones

Scones are light, tender biscuits, best served hot from the oven.

4 cups flour	1 cup cream
2 eggs	1/3 cup butter
1/2 teaspoon salt	1/2 cup sugar
1-1/2 tablespoons baking powder	

Sift the dry ingredients together and cut in butter until crumbly. Add the eggs and cream. Knead the dough for about 45 seconds. Roll out 1/2 inch thick and cut into triangles. Bake at 400 degrees for about 15 minutes. Serve with butter and preserves. (20 servings). Variations: Add raisins, berries, molasses, nuts or dried currants.

Tip: If you don't want to go to all the work of making scones from scratch, pick up a box of scone mix from the supermarket. (I won't tell!)

Filled Pastry Puffs

1 cup flour	4 eggs
1/2 cup softened butter	1 cup water
1/4 cup sugar (optional)	1/2 teaspoon salt

Combine water and butter in a saucepan and bring to a boil. Remove from heat and add the flour, sugar and salt all at once. Stir quickly, forming mixture into a thick, smooth ball. Beat the eggs together thoroughly and add to the ball, a little at a time. Spoon the dough onto greased cookie sheets, about 2 inches apart. Bake at 400 degrees for about 10 minutes, then at 350 degrees for 10 more minutes, until crisp. Fill with chicken, tuna, or shrimp salad, mincemeat pie mix or any fruit pie filling. (25 servings)

Tip: You can save a lot of work by purchasing ready-to-use frozen puff pastry in your supermarket.

Berry Trifle
Now, here's a nice surprise—something that looks spectacular, but takes very little work!

2 large boxes of ladyfingers	Brandy or fruit liqueur
1 large package of frozen raspberries	1 large package of lemon pudding mix
1 jar of apricot preserves	Whipping cream

In a clear glass bowl with high sides, alternate layers of ladyfingers, drizzled with the brandy or liqueur and layers of the preserves, thawed raspberries and prepared pudding. Top with a layer of fruit piled with freshly whipped cream. Refrigerate for at least one hour. (20 servings)

Formal sit-down dinner

Although informality is the trend in wedding showers, a sit-down dinner may be preferable for a formal engagement party. If you like the idea of a formal dinner, but you'd rather not prepare and serve it yourself, you may decide to have it catered so you can relax and enjoy the occasion.

However, if you do decide to prepare and serve the dinner yourself, here is an elegant menu that includes several dishes that can be prepared in advance, which will ease a little of the last minute anxiety, at least. Select from the snack and appetizer menu at the beginning of the last chapter, and consider these recipes for your affair.

Vichyssoise
This elegant French soup is actually quite easy to prepare if you use instant potatoes (no one will ever know!) And, of course, it can be cooked ahead of time and left in your refrigerator until served.

2 small yellow onions, grated	2 tablespoons instant chicken
2 cups water	bouillon
1/2 teaspoon salt	4 cups whole milk
2-1/2 cups instant dry mashed	2 cups cream
potatoes	Chopped chives

Combine onion, bouillon, water and salt in large kettle. Heat to boiling. Reduce heat, cover and simmer for 15 minutes. Remove from heat. Add milk and instant potatoes. Whip until fluffy. Gradually stir in remaining milk and heat *just* to boiling point. Cover and chill in refrigerator. Just before serving, stir in the cold cream, beating vigorously with a fork until blended. Serve topped with chopped chives. (12 servings)

Grapefruit, Melon, Avocado Salad

2 large Crenshaw melons	3 large, ripe avocados
or cantaloupe	2 cans grapefruit pieces
1 cup mayonnaise	1 tablespoon sugar
2 heads butter lettuce	Orange juice, as required to thin
	mayonnaise

Place lettuce leaves on salad plates. Cut melon slices into 1 inch-wide half-moon shapes and arrange three slices on each plate. Drain grapefruit and arrange pieces next to melons. Cover with plastic wrap and chill in refrigerator until ready to serve. Combine mayonnaise, sugar and enough orange juice to form a thin dressing. Chill dressing until ready to serve. Just before serving, slice each avocado into 8 half-moon pieces and arrange them on the salad plates next to the grapefruit, two pieces per plate. Drizzle dressing over the salad before serving. (12 servings)

Fillet of Beef with Mushroom Sauce

6 pounds tenderloin of beef	1 pound bacon

Place bacon strips on top of beef and roast at 325 degrees for approximately 2-1/2 hours (until internal meat thermometer reads 170 degrees.) Cut into thick slices to serve.

Mushroom Sauce:
Add one pound of fresh, sliced sauteed mushrooms to one large bottle of mushroom sauce. Heat thoroughly and pour over top of beef before serving. (12 servings)

Buttered Red Potatoes

12 small red potatoes, peeled and quartered	1/2 cup melted butter
	Chopped parsley

Boil potatoes until tender. Serve covered with butter and parsley. (12 servings)

Asparagus Tips with Hollandaise Sauce
3 pounds frozen asparagus tips
2 bottles Hollandaise sauce

This elegant dish is so easy it's embarrassing! Cook asparagus according to directions on the package. Pour the Hollandaise into your prettiest gravy server and dribble over asparagus as it is served onto guests' plates. (12 servings)

Parker House Rolls
Purchase from your local bakery. Heat before serving.

Dessert
Serve the Heavenly Blueberry Surprise (Chapter 8), but without the melon, since the guests have already had melon in their salads. However, delicate pirouette cookies may be placed in the side of the ice cream or yogurt for a dramatic touch.

Dessert Cheeses
Once the dessert has been served, bring out a tray of dessert cheeses, such as Brie, Camembert, Gouda, Edam, and Gruyere.

After-Dinner Mints and Chocolate Truffles
Visit your local gourmet candy store and splurge on a selection
of their melt-in-the-mouth mints and truffles.

If you really want to impress your guests, present the main
course on an elegantly decorated serving cart that can be rolled
up to each guest for French service, where each plate is indi-
vidually served off a rolling cart in the presence of the guests, as
opposed to plate service where the plates are filled in the kitchen
and brought out two-at-a-time.

Also, an alternative to the formal sit-down dinner might be
a Scandinavian smorgasbord, which is described in the next
chapter. Depending on the setting and the hour of day, it can be
quite a formal affair.

CHAPTER 11

৵

International Cuisine

Food stations may be used to serve any of the international menus in this chapter, except the Scandinavian smorgasbord, which should always be served from one long table.

Italian pasta party

There are two easy ways to host an Italian pasta feast. The first is to make it a potluck affair, asking each guest to bring one hot pasta dish, such as spaghetti, fettuccini, ravioli, cannelloni, lasagna, or stuffed manicotti. All you'll need to provide are an antipasto tray, a green salad, and toasted garlic bread.

Or you can host your own pasta bar that features spaghetti and fettuccini noodles, plus ready-made specialty sauces from the grocery store (in flavors such as tomato and basil, Italian sausage and fennel, mushrooms and ripe olives, roasted peppers and onions, sun-dried tomato, creamy mushroom, etc.). Serve each sauce in its own bowl, with an identifying card propped in front. Your guests will never know you purchased these sauces at your supermarket—unless you tell them, of course! Be sure to serve several types of grated cheeses as well, such as Parmesan, Romano, garlic herb, and zesty red pepper. Of course, you'll also need to add a salad and garlic bread.

Scandinavian smorgasbord

This smorgasbord is suitable for a formal or informal affair:
- Swedish meatballs
- Marinated herring with sour cream sauce
- Marinated anchovy fillets
- Potato sausage ("korv")
- Fish balls
- "Burning Love" potato casserole
- Deviled eggs
- Light and dark dessert breads
- A bowl of fruit balls and berries*
- Havarti cheese
- Swedish macaroon tea cakes

The recipes for the Swedish meatballs, fish balls, "Burning Love" casserole, and the Swedish macaroon tea cakes are provided here. The herring and anchovy fillets are sold in the supermarket, although you may want to add a little more sour cream, a squirt of lemon, and a few capers to the marinated herring before serving. The potato sausage can be ordered through most delicatessens. Traditionally, the fish foods are set at one end of the table and the meats at the other, with the other dishes arranged in between.

"Burning Love" Potato Casserole

4 pounds cooked mashed potatoes	2 teaspoons salt
1/2 teaspoon white pepper	2 pounds canned Danish bacon
4 cups cubed pickled beets	6 medium yellow onions
	Chopped parsley

Dice bacon and onions and sauté in butter until onions are tender. Add seasonings to the mashed potatoes. Place potatoes in large casserole dish, and pour the drained bacon and onions over the top. Bake in 300-degree oven for 10 minutes. Garnish with pickled beets and parsley. (Makes 20 servings.)

Swedish Meatballs

2 pounds ground chuck
1 pound ground pork
2 eggs, slightly beaten
2 tablespoons cornstarch
1 cup hot milk
2 tablespoons flour
1 teaspoon pepper

1/2 cup butter
2 yellow onions, minced
1/2 teaspoon nutmeg
1/2 teaspoon ground ginger
3 teaspoons salt
1/4 teaspoon allspice

Mix meat, eggs, milk, and cornstarch. Add all the rest of the ingredients, except for the flour and butter. Form mixture into small balls and brown in the butter. Add a little water and simmer slowly for about 40 minutes. Remove the meatballs from the pan and make a gravy out of the drippings by adding the flour and enough water for a medium-thick gravy. (Serves 20.)

Fish Balls

4 pounds salmon
1 teaspoon salt
1 teaspoon pepper

1/2 teaspoon nutmeg
1/2 teaspoon mace
Milk and butter as needed

Remove the bones and grind up the salmon with a meat grinder. Add seasonings and enough milk to form the mixture into balls. Fry in butter. (Makes 20 servings.)

Swedish Macaroon Tea Cakes

4 cups sifted flour
2 cups softened butter
1 tablespoon vanilla

1 cup sugar
2 eggs

Cream sugar and butter together, then beat in the eggs and vanilla. Stir in the flour, and mix well. Drop a rounded teaspoonful of batter into each greased tiny muffin cup, pressing batter over the bottom and up around the sides, a coating about 1/4-inch thick. Chill and then fill each hollow with:

Almond Macaroon Filling

4 eggs	1 cup sugar
1 teaspoon almond extract	3 cups finely chopped almonds

Beat eggs until foamy. Add sugar and mix until blended. Add almonds and almond extract. Bake at 325 degrees for about 25 minutes, until browned and set. (Makes 4 dozen tea cakes)

Mexican fiesta

Mexican Nachos

Combine shredded jack cheese and shredded cheddar cheese (3 parts jack to 1 part cheddar) and microwave on high for 2 minutes, stirring halfway through. Serve with large tortilla chips.

Taco Salad

2 pounds ground beef	2 pounds canned red kidney
1/2 teaspoon salt	beans
1/2 teaspoon pepper	1/2 teaspoon garlic powder
1 head lettuce, torn into	2 large tomatoes, cubed
small pieces	3 large avocados, cubed
4 scallions, sliced	1 cup grated cheddar cheese
2 cups crushed tortilla chips	2 cups salsa

Brown beef and drain well. Add drained beans and seasonings, and cook at low heat for 5 minutes. Toss together with the lettuce, tomato, avocado, scallions, cheese, and tortilla chips. Top with salsa and serve. (Serves 12 to 14.)

Chili Salsa Salad

Large bottle medium-hot salsa
1 medium can diced green
  chilies
Crumbled tortilla chips

2 small cans corn (noncreamed)
2 tablespoons lime juice
1 tablespoon chili powder

Mix first 5 ingredients together and chill. Sprinkle with crumbled tortilla chips just before serving.

Taco Picante Casserole*

2 boxes Spanish-flavored rice
  or Mexican-style rice
2 pounds extra lean hamburger
2 7-1/2-ounce cans nonfat
  refried beans
2 small onions, chopped
2 large packages low-fat
  sharp cheddar cheese
2 teaspoons ground cumin
Scallions

4 corn tortillas
1 24-ounce jar medium hot
  picante sauce
6 cloves of garlic, chopped
4 4-ounce cans diced green
  chilies
2 4-ounce cans sliced black
  olives
2 7-ounce cans corn, drained

Prepare the rice according to directions on box. Brown hamburger, garlic, onions, and cumin in a heavy skillet sprayed first with fat-free oil. Drain well on a paper towel and combine with the rice mixture. Prepare 2 round glass casserole dishes with fat-free spray. Cut 6 tortillas into 8 triangles each. Arrange 8 triangles in a pie shape on the bottom of each dish, followed by a layer of the beef mix, beans, whole green chilies, picante sauce, corn, and cheese. Repeat the process, ending with a topping of grated cheese and 8 more tortilla triangles. Finally, garnish with sliced black olives and chopped scallions. Bake at 375 degrees for about 40 minutes, until it is all melted together. Let set for 10 minutes before serving. (Makes 12 to 14 servings.)

Tijuana Tamale Pie

1-1/2 pounds ground beef
5 cups milk
4 beaten eggs
2 7-ounce cans whole
kernel corn
2 14-1/2-ounce cans whole
peeled tomatoes, undrained
and cut up

2 small cans sliced black olives
2-1/4 cups yellow cornmeal
1 pound grated Cheddar cheese
2 teaspoons garlic salt
2 teaspoons chili powder
2 packages taco spices
1 large jar medium hot salsa

Brown ground beef until crumbly, and drain well. In a large bowl combine milk, 2 cups cornmeal, and eggs. Add beef and remaining ingredients, except for the cheese and 1/4 cup of cornmeal. Stir together, and pour into 2 lightly greased 12 x 8 x 2-inch baking dishes. Bake uncovered in 350 degree oven for 40 to 45 minutes. Sprinkle with the cheese and remaining cornmeal; continue baking until cheese melts and cornmeal is browned. Let stand for 10 minutes before serving. Serve with salsa. (Serves 16.)

Mexican Sopaipillas

4 cups flour
4 level teaspoons baking
powder
Shortening for deep frying

2 teaspoons salt
Water
1/4 cup shortening

Sift dry ingredients together. Cut in shortening. Add a little water, just enough to hold dough together. Roll thin, and cut into 2-inch squares or triangles. Fry to a golden brown in deep, *very* hot shortening. They will puff up. Serve hot with butter and honey, or sprinkle with powdered sugar.

Note: These are tricky because unless you fry them in very hot oil or shortening, they will fall flat. Try a batch out ahead of time just to be sure they'll turn out. (Serves 12 to 15.)

Irish fare

Corned Beef and Cabbage

6 pounds well-trimmed corned beef brisket
3 cloves garlic, minced
2 small onions, quartered
1 large head green cabbage, cut into wedges
6 red potatoes, peeled and quartered

Place brisket in large kettle, and cover with cold water. Add garlic and onions. Heat to boiling. Reduce heat, cover tightly, and simmer for 4 hours, or until tender. About 30 minutes before meat is tender, add potatoes to the pot. Remove the meat when it is tender, place on a hot platter, and cover with foil to keep warm while you cook the cabbage. Add cabbage to the kettle, and boil until cabbage and potatoes are tender, about 15 minutes. To serve, surround the brisket with the drained cabbage and potatoes.

Very important: Brisket must be sliced thinly *across* the grain.

Irish Stew

6 lb. lamb roast, cut into 1-inch cubes
8 cups cubed potatoes
1 teaspoon pepper
1/4 cup minced parsley
Mint leaves
2 cups each of cut-up carrots, turnips, celery, yellow onions
2 teaspoons salt
2 bay leaves
1 teaspoon thyme

Roll meat in flour, and brown in hot olive oil. Cover with boiling water, and simmer for 2 hours. Add vegetables and seasonings, and simmer 45 minutes, or until vegetables are tender. Thicken liquid for gravy. Garnish with mint leaves.

Irish Potatoes

The Irish like their potatoes "straight up," boiled in their skins, drained, and served. Small new potatoes are their favorites.

Fruit and Cheese Tray

As I mentioned earlier, any fresh fruit will work, although strawberries, melons, and grapes are popular choices because they hold up well and have a showy appearance. Also, specialty cheeses are very nice, such as Brie, Camembert, Gouda, Edam, and Gruyere.

Irish Appleberry Crunch

1-1/2 pounds apples	1-1/2 pounds blackberries
1/4 cup water	1-1/2 cup sugar
2 sticks butter	2 cups flour
1-1/3 cup oatmeal	1/2 cup dark brown sugar

Peel, core, and slice the apples. Add to washed blackberries, and place in large, shallow baking pan. Dribble the water and sugar over the top. Combine softened butter, flour, oatmeal, and brown sugar in a bowl, and mix together until all the ingredients stick together and become crumbly. Spread these crumbly pieces over the top of the fruit, packing down lightly. Bake in preheated 400-degree oven for 15 minutes. Then reduce heat to 375 degrees, and cook for another 15 to 20 minutes, or until cooked through and crunchy on top. Serve warm with whipped cream or vanilla ice cream. (Serves 16.)

Far East feast

Chinese Cabbage

2 heads cabbage, shredded	1/2 pound butter

Boil cabbage for 5 minutes. Serve topped with melted butter.

Chinese Chicken Salad*

4 whole chicken breasts,
  cut into thin strips
8 scallions, sliced thin
1 teaspoon dry mustard
1/2 teaspoon salt
1/2 cup sesame seeds, toasted
1/3 cup plum sauce

Virgin olive oil
2 heads of lettuce, shredded
1 cup chopped parsley
1 teaspoon sugar
1/2 teaspoon dry ginger
1 cup slivered almonds, toasted

Stirfry chicken strips in 2 tablespoons oil until cooked through. Allow chicken to cool. Toss lettuce, onion, and parsley together in a large salad bowl. Add cooled chicken. Combine 4 tablespoons oil, plum sauce, mustard, sugar, and seasonings. Add to the salad, tossing gently. Garnish with sesame seeds and almonds.

Pork Chow Mein*

4 cups thinly sliced lean,
  boneless pork
3 cups chopped celery
2 cans bean sprouts
1 teaspoon pepper
1/4 cup soy sauce

1 chopped yellow onion
3 cups water
2 teaspoons salt
1/3 cup corn starch
2 tablespoons brown sauce

Spray wok or skillet with cooking spray, and fry pork and onion together until tender. Add celery, salt, pepper, and water. Cook for 20 minutes. Drain. Add bean sprouts, and bring to boil. Make a paste of the corn starch, soy sauce, and brown sauce, and pour it over the mixture, cooking only until thickened. Serve over chow mein noodles.

Shrimp Fried Rice*

3 cups cold cooked rice
1/4 lb. cooked shrimp
2 eggs
1/4 cup sliced water chestnuts

2 tablespoon peanut or olive oil
1/4 cup light soy sauce
3 green onions, chopped
1/2 cup peas

Blend eggs with 2 tablespoons water, and set aside. Heat oil in a wok or heavy skillet over medium heat. Add green onions, and stirfry for 30 seconds. Adds eggs, stirring until firm. Stir in rice, and cook until heated through. Add shrimp, peas, water chestnuts, and soy sauce, stirring until blended and shrimp is heated through.

Fluffy White Rice*
Prepare plain white rice and serve in large bowl.

Pot Stickers
Purchase them in bulk from the freezer section at your supermarket. They are easy to prepare—just steam them in a heavy skillet.

Personalized Fortune Cookies
Order personalized fortune cookies from Creative Cookie, Inc. or serve regular fortune cookies.

Note: Of course, you can always order "take-out," especially if you're short on time. (That's what I *always* do!)

German Oktoberfest

Lentil Soup
4 cups dried lentils
Large ham bone
2 large yellow onions, minced
1/4 cup each butter and flour
   for thickening (if desired)

6 stalks celery, chopped
2 sprigs parsley
1 teaspoon each salt and pepper

Soak lentils in water overnight. Place lentils, ham bone, onion, celery, parsley, and seasonings in large kettle, covered by 6 quarts of water. Bring to a boil, cover, and simmer for about 5 hours, until lentils are tender. Thicken, if desired, with 1/4 cup butter and 1/4 cup flour. (Makes 16 servings.)

Fried Bratwurst

Fry the bratwurst in butter, turning frequently until golden brown on all sides. Cover the bratwurst with water, and simmer uncovered for 20 minutes. Serve with hot mustard or sour cream.

Sauerbraten

4 pounds lean boneless top round beef steak, cut with the grain into 2 inch strips, then cut across the grain into 1/4 inch-thick slanting slices

1 cup each dry white wine and white vinegar
1 teaspoon each pepper and ground cloves
4 cups thinly sliced carrots
4 cloves garlic, minced
1 cup crushed ginger snaps
1/4 cup dark brown sugar
4 dry bay leaves
1/4 cup salad oil
4 red onions, thinly sliced
2 cups thinly sliced celery
1/2 cup water
sour cream, optional

In a bowl, mix wine, vinegar, brown sugar, bay leaf, pepper, and cloves. Stir in meat, and let marinate for 1 hour. Drain meat, reserving marinade. Remove bay leaves. Place wok or heavy skillet over high heat. Add oil. When oil is hot, add meat and stirfry until meat is browned (about 2 minutes). Remove meat, and add onion and carrots. Stirfry for 1 minute. Add celery and garlic. Stirfry for 1 minute. Add water, cover, and cook until carrots and celery are tender, about 3 more minutes. Return meat to wok, and add marinade and ginger snaps. Stir until sauce thickens. Serve garnished with dollops of sour cream. (Serves 16.)

Hot German Potato Salad

12 medium potatoes, boiled in skins, peeled, and sliced thin
1 teaspoon celery seed
1 teaspoon pepper
1-1/2 cups water
1 cup vinegar
14 slices of crumbled bacon
1-1/2 cup diced yellow onion
1/4 cup flour
1/4 cup sugar
3 teaspoons salt
1 tablespoon chopped chives

Cook onion in bacon fat. Mix in all dry ingredients. Add water and vinegar, and cook until mixture boils. Simmer for 3 minutes. Pour over potatoes. Add most of the bacon pieces. Cover and let stand until ready to serve. Garnish with remaining bacon and minced chives. (Serves 12.)

Sauerkraut
Purchase canned or fresh deli sauerkraut.

Fruit and Cheese Tray
(Described under Irish fare.)

Chapter 12

ॐ

Festive Party Drinks

Everyone loves a festive party drink, especially if it has a clever name. In addition to any wines, champagnes, or other alcoholic drinks that will be served during your party, you may want to consider some of these trendy party potables.

California smoothies

Smoothies are a frosty-cold blend of fruits, juices, yogurt, or sorbet that are prepared in a blender. In addition to those basics, "smoothie chefs" customize their recipes with almost anything you can think of, from brownies to tofu. A smoothie is considered to be more healthful than a milkshake and more substantial than a lemonade—the trendy new drink of the decade. *Newsweek* magazine, in fact, has declared it to be the "new cool brew" and predicts it will become as popular as specialty coffees.

The ingredients listed in each of the smoothie recipes in this chapter should be blended together to make one large smoothie. Garnish the drinks with a wedge of orange, lime, pineapple, peach or mango.

The Inner Child Smoothie
1 cup frozen vanilla yogurt
1/2 cup apple juice
1/2 cup peanut butter
1/2 cup honey

Strawberry Monkey
1 cup frozen strawberry yogurt
1/2 cup fresh strawberries
1 banana
1 cup orange juice

Minty Zinger
1 cucumber, peeled, seeded,
  and chopped
1 cup apple cider
1/2 cup crushed ice
2 tablespoons finely chopped
  mint leaves
1 cup lemon sorbet

Smooth Tango
8 apricots, pitted and chopped
3 small peeled, sliced tangerines
1/2 cup frozen vanilla yogurt
1 tablespoon sugar

Classic Papaya Smoothie
1 cup peeled, seeded, and
  chopped cantaloupe
1 papaya, peeled, seeded,
  and chopped
1 cup freshly squeezed orange
  juice
1/2 cup frozen vanilla yogurt

Mango Surprise
1 chilled mango, peeled and
  chopped
1 teaspoon ground cardamom
1/2 cup crushed ice
1-1/2 cup frozen vanilla yogurt
1 cup chilled fresh pineapple
  chunks

The Healthy Berry
1 cup frozen vanilla yogurt
1 cup blackberries
1 cup raspberries
1/2 cup apple juice

Festive fruit drinks

Peachy Sunset

3/4 cup peach nectar
1 tablespoon lime juice
3 tablespoons grenadine syrup

1 peach, pitted and sliced
 (*not* peeled)
1-1/2 cups ice

Process the ice, nectar, peace slices, and lime juice in a juicer. Pour grenadine into bottom of each glass. Pour blended mixture on top. (Syrup will send brilliant streaks to the top of the glass, creating a "peachy sunset.")

Black and Blue Slushie

2 large apples, cut into wedges
1-1/2 cups blueberries

2-1/2 cups blackberries
Whipped cream

Process the three fruits in a juicer, and serve with a dollop of whipped cream on top.

Sweet Shamrock

1-1/2 cups Thompson seedless
 green grapes

2 pears, cut into wedges
3 plums, pitted and cut into
 wedges

Process the fruits in a juicer. Garnish with a slice of lime.

The Tex-Mex

4 large tomatoes, cut into
 wedges
3 jalapeño peppers, stemmed
1 teaspoon celery salt

1 medium cucumber, peeled
 and cut into wedges
2 teaspoons horseradish
2 teaspoons Worcestershire
 sauce

Process all the ingredients together in a juicer.

Silky Strawberry

12 large strawberries
1 small apple, cut into wedges
whipped cream

1/2 small cantaloupe, peeled
and chopped

Process the strawberries, cantaloupe, and apple together in a juicer. Serve topped with whipped cream.

Moonbeam

1/2 honeydew melon, peeled,
seeded, and chopped
1 cup ginger ale

1 apricot, pitted and chopped
2 peaches, pitted and chopped

Blend the fruits together until smooth. Add the ginger ale, and mix very gently.

Tropical Mango

3 mangoes, peeled, pitted and
cut into wedges

1 cup raspberries
1 cup chopped, fresh pineapple

Process fruits together in a juicer.

Kiwi Refresher

2 kiwi, peeled and cut into
wedges
1 cup freshly squeezed
grapefruit juice

1 large peach, pitted and
cut into wedges
1/4 cup freshly squeezed
lime juice

Process the kiwi and peach in a juicer. Add grapefruit and lime juice, and mix well.

"Pleased as punch" recipes

Sangria Punch

1 gallon red wine	4 oranges, sliced and quartered
4 apples, peeled, cored, and sliced	1/2 lemon, sliced
	1-1/2 cups sugar
2 tablespoons cinnamon	1 cup light rum

Mix ingredients together in a large crock, glass, or plastic container, and store overnight in a cool place. Do not refrigerate. Just before serving add a block of ice.

Egg Nog Punch

12 egg yolks	1 pound powdered sugar
1 quart dark rum or brandy	2-1/2 quarts whipping cream
1 quart whole milk	6 egg whites
1/2 teaspoon salt	Freshly grated nutmeg

Beat egg yolks until light in color. Beat in powdered sugar, liquor, cream, and milk. Cover and refrigerate for at least 4 hours. Beat egg whites until stiff, and fold lightly with the salt, and combine with the chilled mixture. Top each serving with freshly grated nutmeg.

Creamy Mocha Punch

1 cup instant coffee granules	2 gallons whole milk
4 cups hot water	1 gallon vanilla ice cream
3 cups sugar	1 gallon chocolate ice cream
1 quart whipped cream	

Combine the coffee, water, and sugar, and set in the refrigerator for 1 hour. Set the 2 gallons of ice cream out to soften 15 minutes before serving time. Combine half the cooled coffee mixture, ice cream, and milk. Spread half the whipped cream evenly over the top of the punch and serve. (Return the rest of the ingredients to the refrigerator or freezer to use to refill the punch bowl.)

Wassail Bowl

5 medium baking apples	1 cup sugar
1/4 cup water	3 cups ale
3-1/2 cups apple cider	1 teaspoon allspice

Core apples, and sprinkle with 1/2 cup sugar. Add water and bake at 375 degrees for 30 minutes, or until tender. Combine ale, cider, remaining sugar, and allspice in saucepan, and place over low heat. Stir until sugar is dissolved, but do not boil. Place roasted apples in punch bowl, and pour ale mixture over them.

Cranberry Punch

5 tea bags	5 cups boiling water
1/2 teaspoon allspice	1/2 teaspoon cinnamon
1/2 teaspoon nutmeg	1 cup sugar
1 quart cranberry juice	3 cups water
1 cup orange juice	3/4 cup lemon juice

Pour boiling water over tea bags and the spices and steep for 5 minutes. Strain, add sugar, and let cool. Add cranberry juice, water, orange, and lemon juice, and mix. Pour into punch bowl with ice cubes made from lemon juice. Float thin lemon slices on top of the punch.

Polynesian Volcano Punch

1 gallon cold fruit punch	2 cups guava juice
2 bottles cold ginger ale or lemon-lime soda	1/2 gallon rainbow sherbet

Mix the fruit punch and guava juice together, then add the sherbet. Pour the ginger ale or lemon-lime directly on top of the sherbet, which will make the punch foam like a "volcano."

Tip: Don't add plain ice to your punch because it will water it down. Add frozen juice instead. (Freeze ahead in circular gelatin molds or in ice cube trays).

Specialty coffee drinks

Cafe au Rhum
Add 1 ounce rum and a twist of lemon peel per cup.

Cafe Cacao
Add 1 ounce creme de cacao per cup.

Cafe a L'Orange
Add 1 ounce Orange Curaçao per cup with a cinnamon stick to stir.

Cafe Mocha
Equal amounts of coffee and hot chocolate topped with whipped cream.

Irish Coffee
Add 1 ounce Irish whiskey and 3 teaspoons of sugar. Top with whipped cream.

Cafe Cappuccino
Equal amounts of espresso and hot milk. Add two teaspoons sugar and sprinkles of cinnamon and nutmeg. (Or you can use instant cappuccino mix.)

Caffe Borgia
Equal amounts of espresso and hot chocolate, served in a demi-tasse cup, topped with whipped cream and grated orange peel.

Coffee a la Mode
Add a couple of tablespoons vanilla or coffee ice cream to the coffee just before you serve it.

Festive dessert drinks

Cappuccino Float

Pour 3 or 4 tablespoons of chocolate syrup in the bottom of a tall clear glass. Add 1 crumbled cookie* and 1 scoop chocolate ice cream. Pour iced cappuccino** over the ice cream, to within an inch of the top of the glass. Add a small scoop of praline ice cream, a squirt of whipped cream and another cookie, which should be stuck into the side of the praline ice cream.

    *   Pepperidge Farm Chocolate Laced Pirouettes Cookies (delicate "rolled" cookies that look like tiny stovepipes)

  ** Use any instant cappuccino mix.

Rooty-Tooty Float
Vanilla ice cream
Chilled root beer
Whipped cream

This is your classic root beer float, except that you use *real* ice cream (not ice milk or low-fat ice cream), and you top it with a generous scoop of whipped cream.

❧PART III❧

Putting It All Down on Paper

The worksheets that follow have been created to help you:
• Know what to do and when to do it.
• Stay organized.
• Establish your party budget.

But these worksheets won't do you a bit of good if you don't use them. The biggest mistake you can make is to try to keep track of everything in your head. Take it from me: If you want the planning to be easy and successful, don't trust your memory. Although a brain isn't a computer, it *is* known to get overloaded and start "dropping data" from time to time—especially when it's under stress. So get in the habit of using these worksheets as you plan.

By the way, feel free to take these worksheets to a copy center where they can be enlarged to fit a three-ring notebook, in which you could also store several plastic zipper pouch inserts for saving receipts, sample invitations, ribbon samples, party recipes, and so forth. This notebook will be a valuable tool to keep you on track and make your party the easiest and most successful one you've every hosted.

CHAPTER 13

ॐ

The Ultimate Shower Scheduler

This timetable will help you with your party planning. Use the left-hand column to record the date each task is completed.

Timetable

Things to complete several weeks in advance:

Date Completed	Task
_____	Enlist a co-host and/or volunteers to help with the party.
_____	Confer with your guest(s) of honor regarding a convenient date and time for the party.
_____	Choose a location for the party.
_____	Choose a theme.
_____	Create or purchase invitations.
_____	Assemble a guest list and address and mail invitations.
_____	Plan a menu, including detailed recipes and a list of food that can be prepared or purchased in advance and placed in the freezer.
_____	Place order with deli or caterer, if necessary.
_____	Place order with bakery (for rolls, cake, etc.).
_____	Plan the entertainment, including games, music, and toasts.
_____	Make or purchase favors.
_____	Make or purchase prizes.
_____	Make or purchase name tags.
_____	Make or purchase place cards.
_____	Create, purchase, borrow, or rent decorations.
_____	Purchase film or single-use cameras.

	Assemble and clean all crystal, china, silver, linens, etc.
_____	
_____	Decide what outfit you're going to wear to the party and have it ready to wear (including accessories).
_____	Other:
_____	Other:
_____	Other:
_____	Other:

◆

Things to be done two weeks in advance:

Date Completed	Task
_____	Place order with your florist for the corsage for the bride, boutonniere for the groom, and corsages for any mothers or grandmothers who will be attending, plus a centerpiece and any other floral arrangements.
_____	Other:
_____	Other:
_____	Other:

Things to be done one week in advance:

Date Completed	Task
_____	Call any guests who have not responded to your RSVP to see if they are coming.
_____	Based on the responses to your RSVPs, start filling out the name tags and place cards.
_____	If you have an ice maker, empty it frequently into plastic bags and store them in your freezer. Otherwise, purchase plenty of ice ahead of time.
_____	Other:

◆

Things to be done a few days before the party:

Date Completed	Task
	If the party is being held in your home:
_____	Clean house.
_____	Stock the guest bathroom with hand towels, lotion, guest soaps, potpourri, a candle, etc.
_____	Call your co-host(s) and volunteers to confirm their duties, including the "little things," such as: *Who will record the gifts as they are opened? Who will create a "pretend bridal bouquet" from the ribbons as the gifts are opened? Who can arrive early to help with last-minute crises? Who can arrive early to help greet the guests?*
_____	Other:

Things to be done two days before the party:

Date Completed	Task
_____	Shop for perishable food items and prepare them as far ahead of time as you can (dicing, marinating, rinsing lettuce, etc.).
_____	Pick up anything you're borrowing or renting for the party (coffee urn, punch bowl, chairs, etc.).
_____	Pick up any rented or borrowed decorations, and start decorating your site.
_____	Call to confirm your floral order and the time of delivery. (Request early-morning delivery on the day of the party.)
_____	Call to confirm bakery order and time it will be ready to be picked up.
_____	Call to confirm deli or catering arrangements, if applicable.
_____	Call your guest(s) of honor and any helpers to confirm their time of arrival.
_____	If the guests will be wearing coats or jackets, clear out your coat closet and fill it with empty hangers.
_____	Other:
_____	Other:
_____	Other:

Things to be done the day of the party:

Date Completed	Task
_____	Last-minute cooking or baking.
_____	Ask one of your helpers to pick up your bakery order.
_____	Ask one of your helpers to pick up your deli order.
_____	Ask one of your helpers to pick up any borrowed or rented decoration items.
_____	Last-minute decorating, including fresh flowers for the guest bathroom and any exterior decorations.
_____	If you will be serving a sit-down meal, arrange the place cards in a clever way so the guests are forced to sit next to someone they don't know. (Be sure to separate spouses.)
_____	If you will be serving food from a buffet table, scatter TV trays around the room or provide lap trays for the guests.
_____	If you plan to serve snacks or appetizers, set them out before your guests are scheduled to arrive.
_____	Other:
_____	Other:
_____	Other:

CHAPTER 14

❧

Wedding Shower "Detail Central"

These easy-to-use planning sheets are self-explanatory and are guaranteed to keep track of every detail—and keep *you* organized!

Master planning sheet

Name(s) of guest(s) of honor	
Name(s) of co-host(s), if applicable	
Date of party	
Time of party	
Location of party	
Party's theme	
Date invitations mailed	
Type of food to be served	

Games, activities, and entertainment

Guest list

Name	Address	Telephone	Replies? Yes	No

Guest list, page 2

Name	Address	Telephone	Replies? Yes	No

Total number of guests attending: ____

Volunteers

Name	Telephone	Duty

*Party site information**

Name and location of site	
Date and time site is available	
Is this my preferred time?	
Name of contact person	
Telephone number	
Site rental fee	
Amount of deposit and date given	
Amount still due and date due	
Other fees (custodial, parking, coat check, etc.)	
Equipment and supplies available (tables, chairs, utensils, coffee pot, pots, pans, linens, dishes, etc.)	
What I will need to provide	
Restrictions (smoking, alcohol, loud music, bringing in food)	
Parking facilities—location and cost	

Total cost of site: $ _____

Transfer amount to the master budget sheet in Chapter 15.
*Photocopy one sheet for each site.

Party decorations

Item	Source	Cost
Flowers		
Balloons		
Streamers		
Baskets		
Candles		
Crepe paper		
Banners		
Acetate/fabric bows		
Tiny white light strands		
Tulle netting		
Novelty decorations		
Other		

Total: _____

Transfer this amount to the master budget in Chapter 15.

Table decorations

Item	Source	Cost
Centerpiece		
Tablecloth		
Napkins		
Napkin rings		
Candles		
Cups/glassware		
Plates		
Utensils		
Place cards		
Favors		
Novelty decorations		

Total: _____
Transfer this amount to the master budget in Chapter 15.

Game supplies

Item	Source	Cost
Supplies	Name of game #1	
Supplies	Name of game #2	
Supplies	Name of game #3	
	Prizes (Including door prizes)	

Total: _____

Transfer this amount to the master budget in Chapter 15.

Party Menu

Snacks and appetizers		
Item	**To be prepared by**	**Cost**

Soups		
Item	**To be prepared by**	**Cost**

Salads		
Item	**To be prepared by**	**Cost**

Sandwiches

Item	To be prepared by	Cost

Meat dishes

Item	To be prepared by	Cost

Side dishes

Item	To be prepared by	Cost

Breads

Item	To be prepared by	Cost

Condiments

Item	To be prepared by	Cost

Desserts

Item	To be prepared by	Cost

Drinks

Item	To be prepared by	Cost

Candies

Item	To be prepared by	Cost

Other

Item	To be prepared by	Cost

Total cost of party menu: _____

Transfer this amount to the master budget in Chapter 15.

Entertainment

Type	Provided by	Cost

Total: _____

Transfer this amount to the master budget in Chapter 15.

Party rentals

Item	Source *with address and telephone*	Cost

Total: _____

Transfer this amount to the master budget in Chapter 15.

My personalized engagement toast

_____

_____

_____

_____

_____

_____

_____

_____

_____

_____

_____

Wording for the invitation

CHAPTER 15

❧

Shower Money Minder

The more you spend on a party doesn't necessarily mean the more fun it will be. You need to decide how much money you have available for hosting the party and then stay within that budget. If you're high on party spirit but low on party funds, here are a few suggestions:

- Hold the party in your home or any other gratis location.
- Ask others to co-host the party with you and share the financial load. One way to do this is to hold a progressive dinner (see Chapter 2).
- Choose one of the more affordable themes, such as a family treasures shower or a junk drawer shower (see Chapter 2).
- Serve punch or soft drinks instead of alcoholic beverages.
- Decorate with things you already have around the house, items that can be borrowed, or "big bangs for the buck" (balloons, crepe paper streamers, etc.).
- Plan a get-together for which everyone pays their own way, such as the amusement park party.

- Buy balloons in bulk from a party supplies store, and rent your own helium tank for blowing them up.
- Send informal invitations, or invite people by word of mouth.
- Choose a theme that requires an affordable menu, such as a progressive dinner, or serve only dessert and coffee.
- Purchase food in bulk from a wholesale food supplier.
- Call the career placement center at your local college or university to locate students to help you prepare and serve the food at a fraction of the cost of a professional caterer.
- Or call your local technical college or vocational school to hire students who are training to become caterers, bakers, etc. (They may even earn school credit by helping you with your party.)

Master Budget

Transfer the total costs for each category from the worksheets in Chapter 14 to this "master budget."

Master Budget

Category	Amount Budgeted	Final Cost	Who Pays?
Rental of party site			
Party decorations			
Table decorations			
Game supplies			
Food			
Entertainment			
Party rentals			
Other:			
Other:			
Other:			
Other:			

Total final cost:_____

꙳

Note Pages

As you plan your party, use these pages to quickly record details you don't want to forget—important names, dates, phone numbers, ordering information, and theme, game, decorating, or entertainment ideas.

Notes

Notes

Notes

_____

_____

_____

_____

_____

_____

_____

_____

_____

_____

_____

_____

Notes

Notes

_____

_____

_____

_____

_____

_____

_____

_____

_____

_____

_____

Notes

Notes

Notes

Epilogue

As you launch into your party plans, here are three final pieces of advice:

1. Don't be shy about asking friends to help you plan the party.
2. Once the party begins, keep it moving. Don't give it a chance to get boring!
3. Relax and enjoy your party—and don't forget to smile!

Good luck,

Diane Warner

P.S. I will be updating this book from time to time and would love to hear about any interesting wedding showers you may have planned or attended. Please write to me in care of my publisher:

Diane Warner
c/o Career Press, Inc.
P. O. Box 687
Franklin Lakes, NJ 07417

Index